For Better or For Worse:®
Grandpas Are for Jumping On

Lynn Johnston

TOR®

A TOM DOHERTY ASSOCIATES BOOK
NEW YORK

FOR BETTER OR FOR WORSE: GRANDPAS ARE FOR JUMPING ON

A Tor Book
Published by Tom Doherty Associates, Inc.
175 Fifth Avenue
New York, N.Y. 10010

ISBN: 0-812-52273-7

First Tor edition: September 1990

Printed in the United States of America

0 9 8 7 6 5 4 3 2

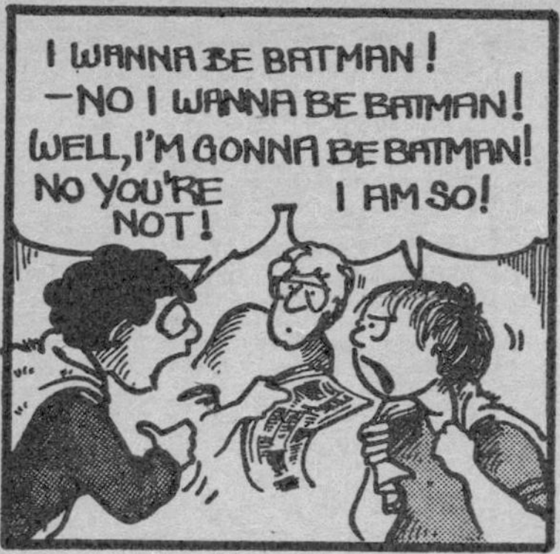
I WANNA BE BATMAN!
-NO I WANNA BE BATMAN!
WELL, I'M GONNA BE BATMAN!
NO YOU'RE NOT!
I AM SO!

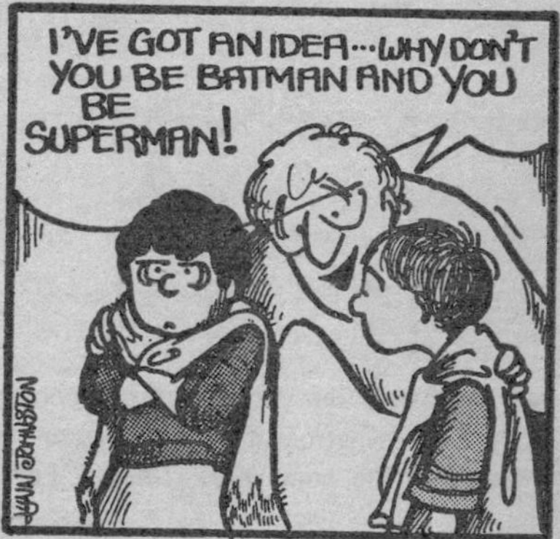
I'VE GOT AN IDEA...WHY DON'T YOU BE BATMAN AND YOU BE SUPERMAN!

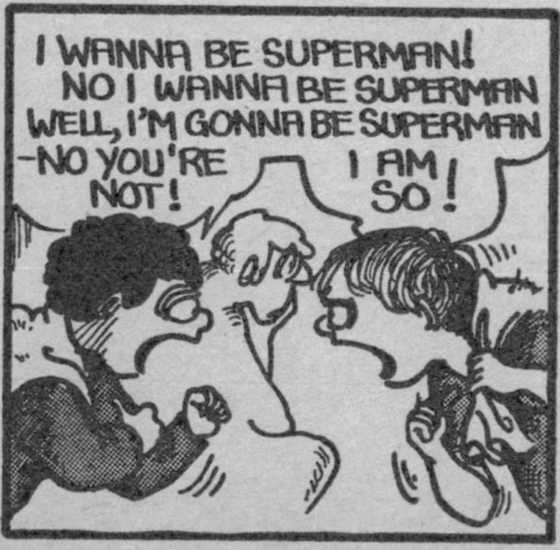
I WANNA BE SUPERMAN!
NO I WANNA BE SUPERMAN
WELL, I'M GONNA BE SUPERMAN
-NO YOU'RE NOT!
I AM SO!

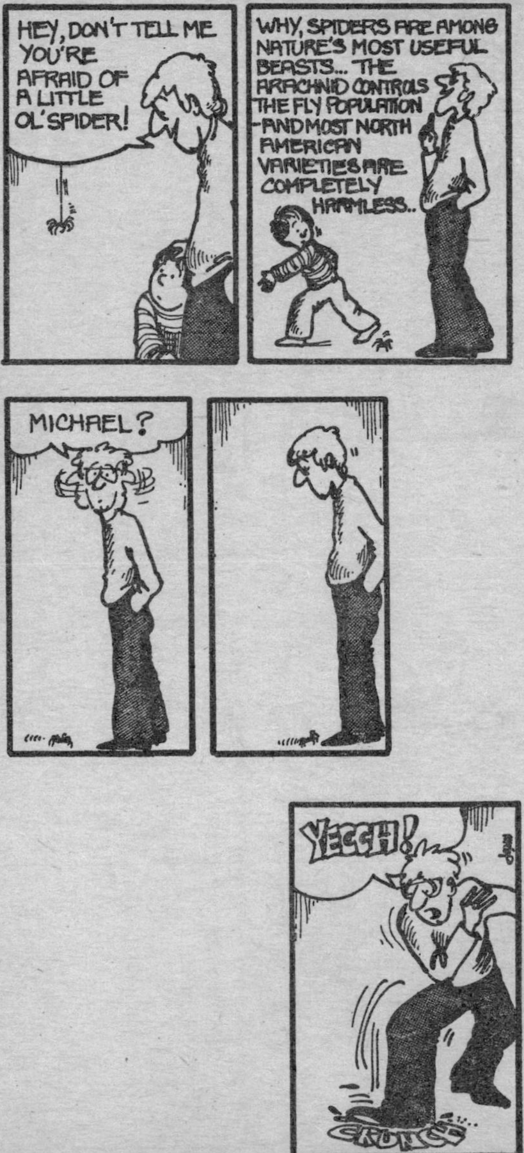
HEY, DON'T TELL ME YOU'RE AFRAID OF A LITTLE OL' SPIDER!
WHY, SPIDERS ARE AMONG NATURE'S MOST USEFUL BEASTS... THE ARACHNID CONTROLS THE FLY POPULATION -AND MOST NORTH AMERICAN VARIETIES ARE COMPLETELY HARMLESS..
MICHAEL?
YECCH!
CRUNCH

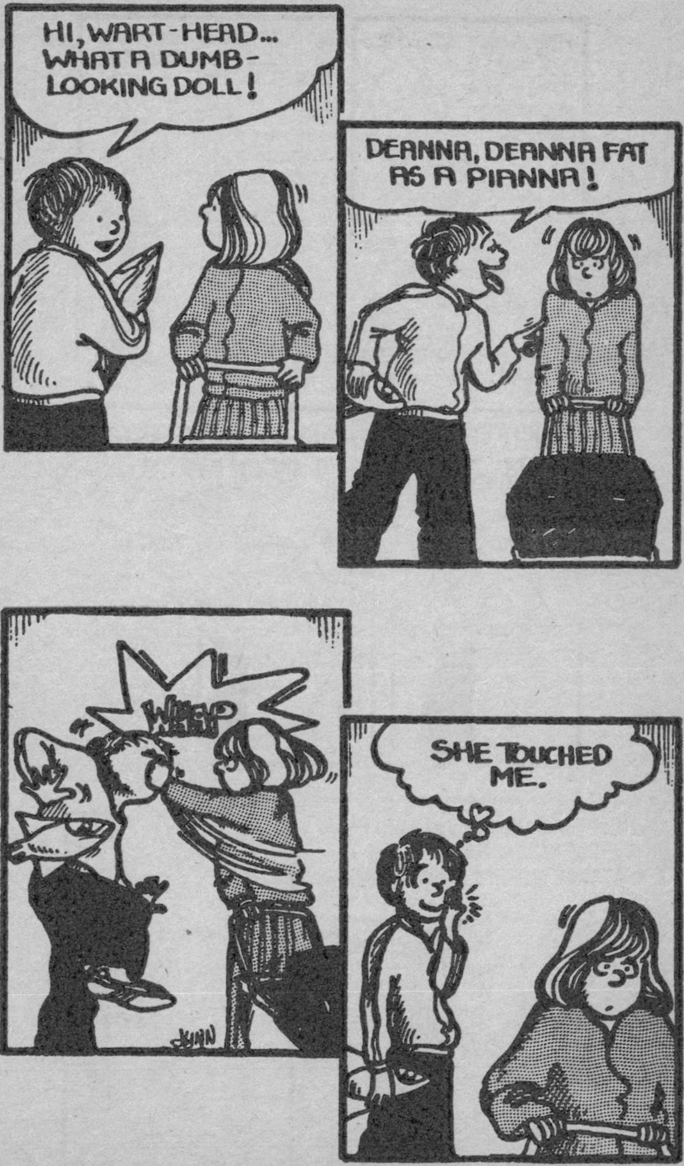
HI, WART-HEAD... WHAT A DUMB-LOOKING DOLL!
DEANNA, DEANNA FAT AS A PIANNA!
SHE TOUCHED ME.

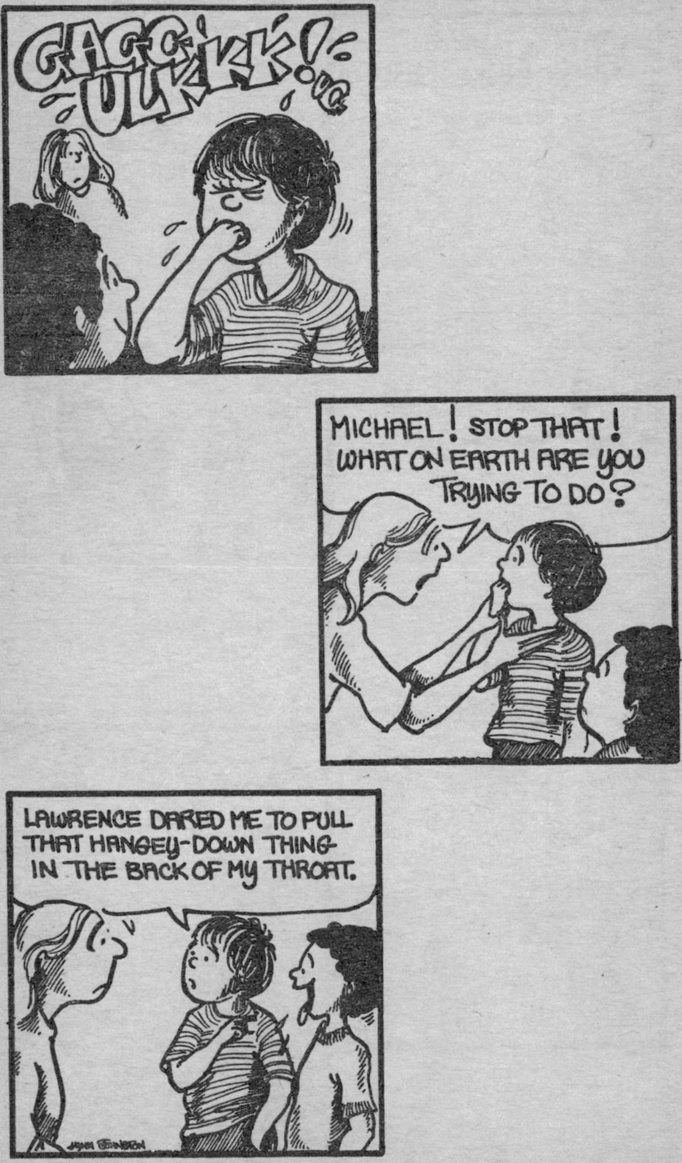
GAGG-ULKKK!
MICHAEL! STOP THAT! WHAT ON EARTH ARE YOU TRYING TO DO?
LAWRENCE DARED ME TO PULL THAT HANGEY-DOWN THING IN THE BACK OF MY THROAT.

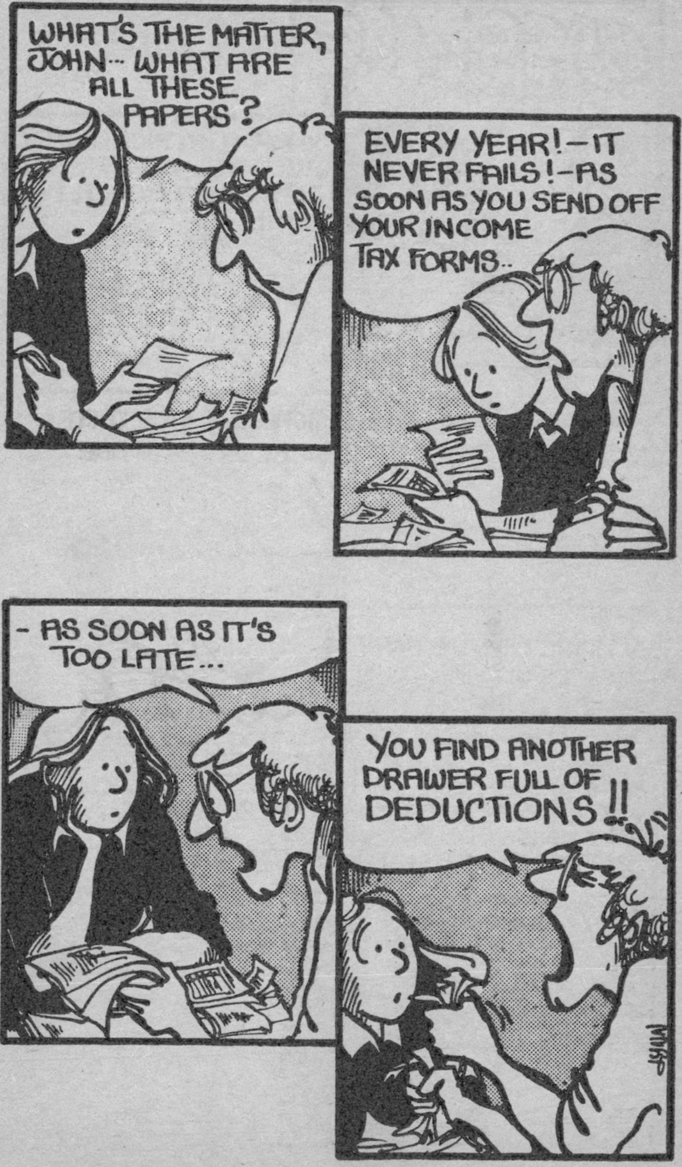
WHAT'S THE MATTER, JOHN... WHAT ARE ALL THESE PAPERS ?
EVERY YEAR!—IT NEVER FAILS!—AS SOON AS YOU SEND OFF YOUR INCOME TAX FORMS..
- AS SOON AS IT'S TOO LATE...
YOU FIND ANOTHER DRAWER FULL OF DEDUCTIONS !!

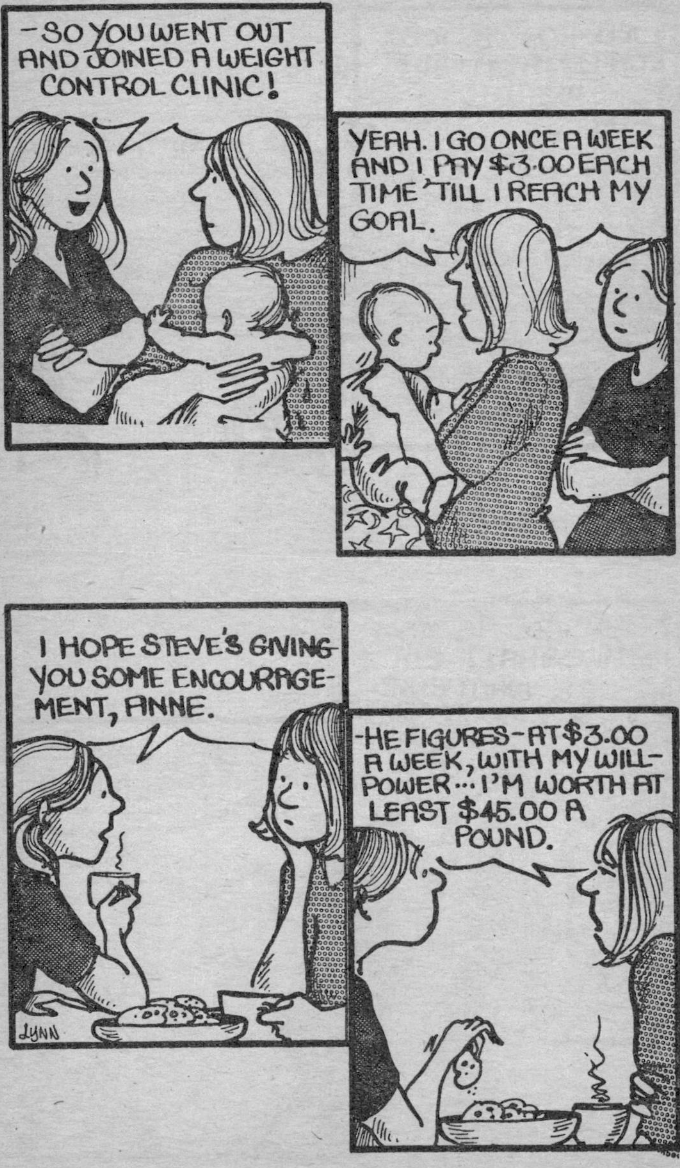
-SO YOU WENT OUT AND JOINED A WEIGHT CONTROL CLINIC!
YEAH. I GO ONCE A WEEK AND I PAY $3.00 EACH TIME 'TILL I REACH MY GOAL.
I HOPE STEVE'S GIVING YOU SOME ENCOURAGE-MENT, ANNE.
-HE FIGURES-AT $3.00 A WEEK, WITH MY WILL-POWER... I'M WORTH AT LEAST $45.00 A POUND.
LYNN

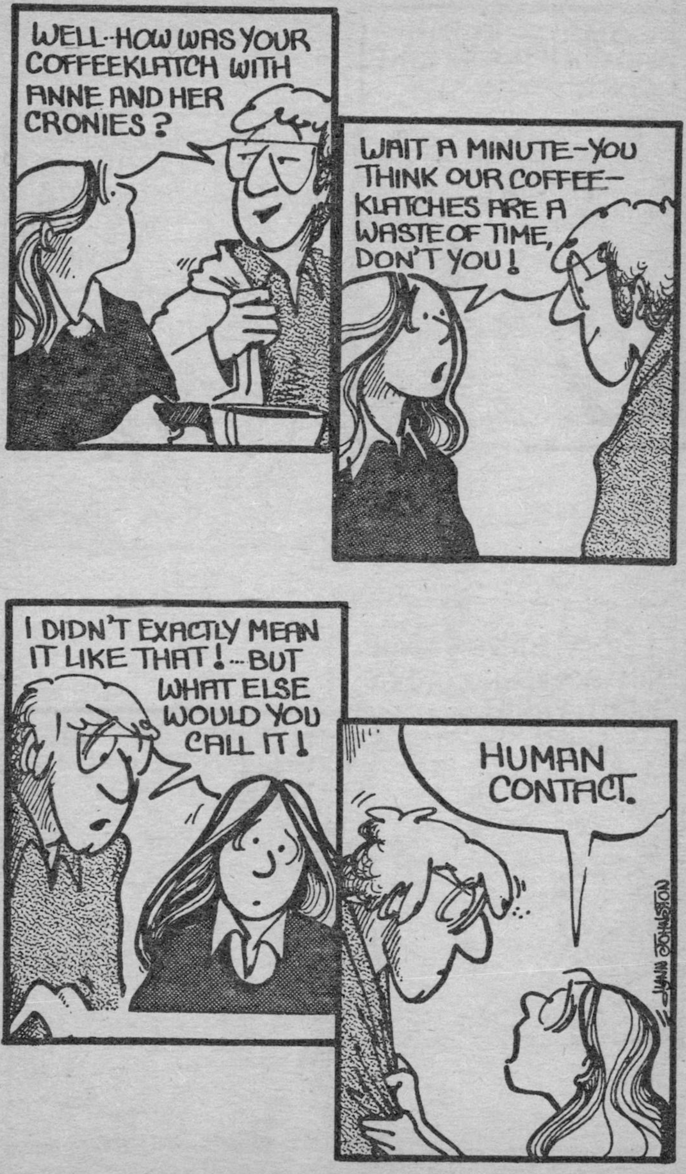
WELL--HOW WAS YOUR COFFEEKLATCH WITH ANNE AND HER CRONIES?
WAIT A MINUTE—YOU THINK OUR COFFEE-KLATCHES ARE A WASTE OF TIME, DON'T YOU!
I DIDN'T EXACTLY MEAN IT LIKE THAT!—BUT WHAT ELSE WOULD YOU CALL IT!
HUMAN CONTACT.
LYNN JOHNSTON

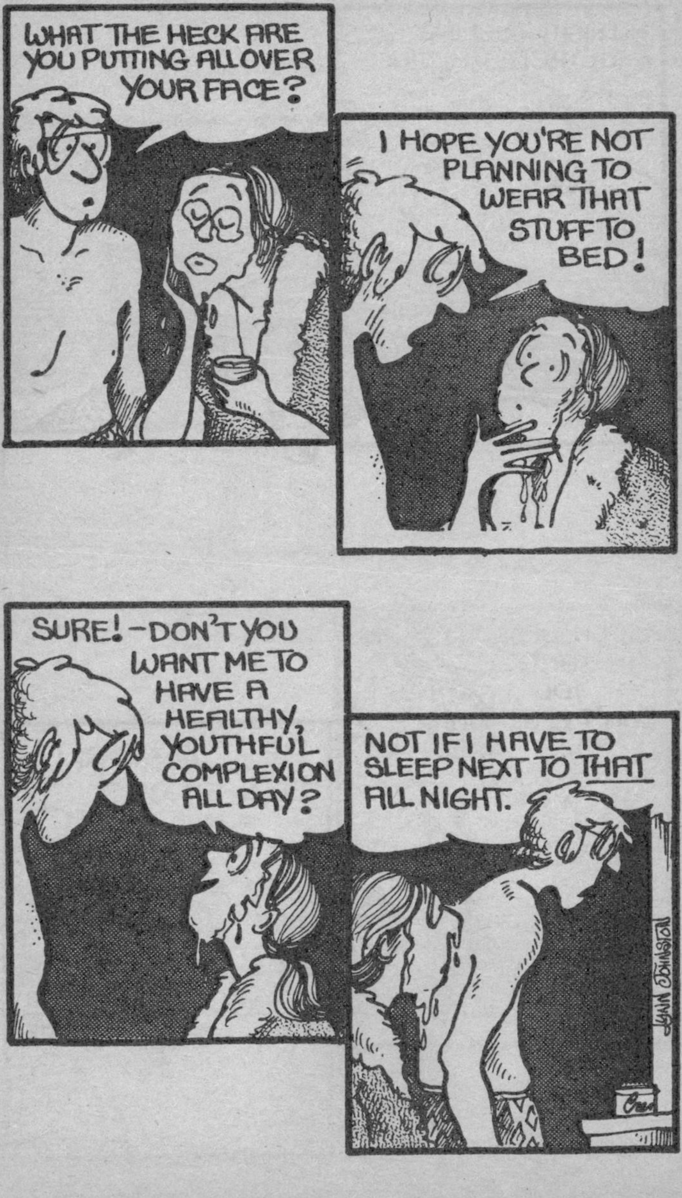
WHAT THE HECK ARE YOU PUTTING ALL OVER YOUR FACE?
I HOPE YOU'RE NOT PLANNING TO WEAR THAT STUFF TO BED!
SURE! -DON'T YOU WANT ME TO HAVE A HEALTHY, YOUTHFUL COMPLEXION ALL DAY?
NOT IF I HAVE TO SLEEP NEXT TO THAT ALL NIGHT.

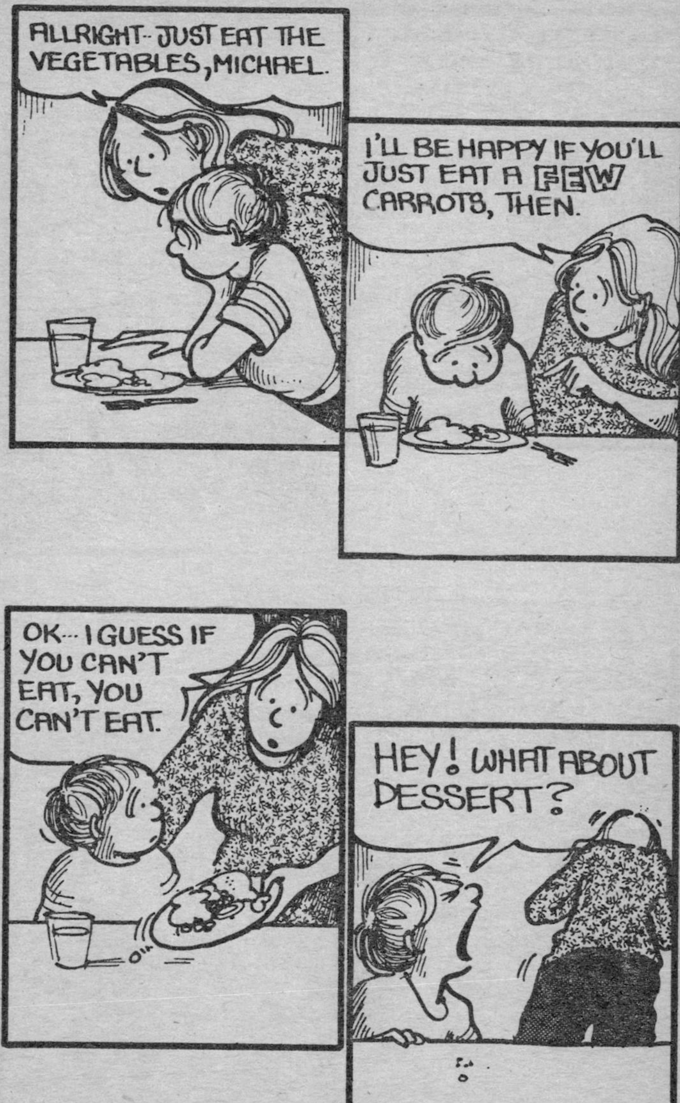
ALLRIGHT-- JUST EAT THE VEGETABLES, MICHAEL.
I'LL BE HAPPY IF YOU'LL JUST EAT A FEW CARROTS, THEN.
OK--- I GUESS IF YOU CAN'T EAT, YOU CAN'T EAT.
HEY! WHAT ABOUT DESSERT?
LYNN JOHNSTON

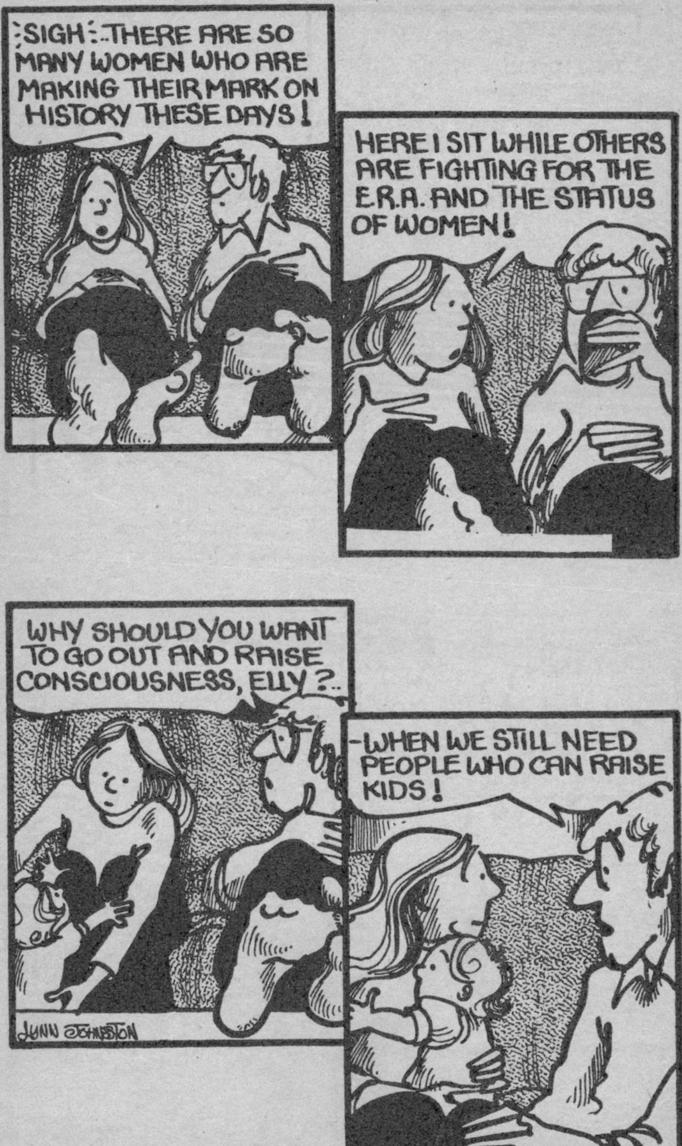
SIGH...THERE ARE SO MANY WOMEN WHO ARE MAKING THEIR MARK ON HISTORY THESE DAYS!
HERE I SIT WHILE OTHERS ARE FIGHTING FOR THE E.R.A. AND THE STATUS OF WOMEN!
WHY SHOULD YOU WANT TO GO OUT AND RAISE CONSCIOUSNESS, ELLY?..
-WHEN WE STILL NEED PEOPLE WHO CAN RAISE KIDS!
LYNN JOHNSTON

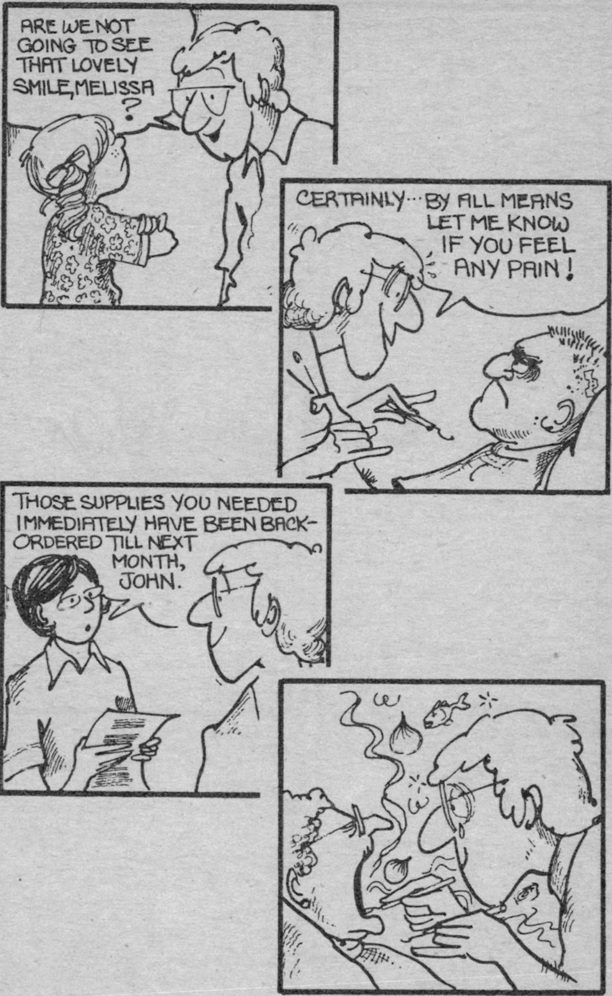
ARE WE NOT GOING TO SEE THAT LOVELY SMILE, MELISSA ?
CERTAINLY... BY ALL MEANS LET ME KNOW IF YOU FEEL ANY PAIN !
THOSE SUPPLIES YOU NEEDED IMMEDIATELY HAVE BEEN BACK-ORDERED TILL NEXT MONTH, JOHN.

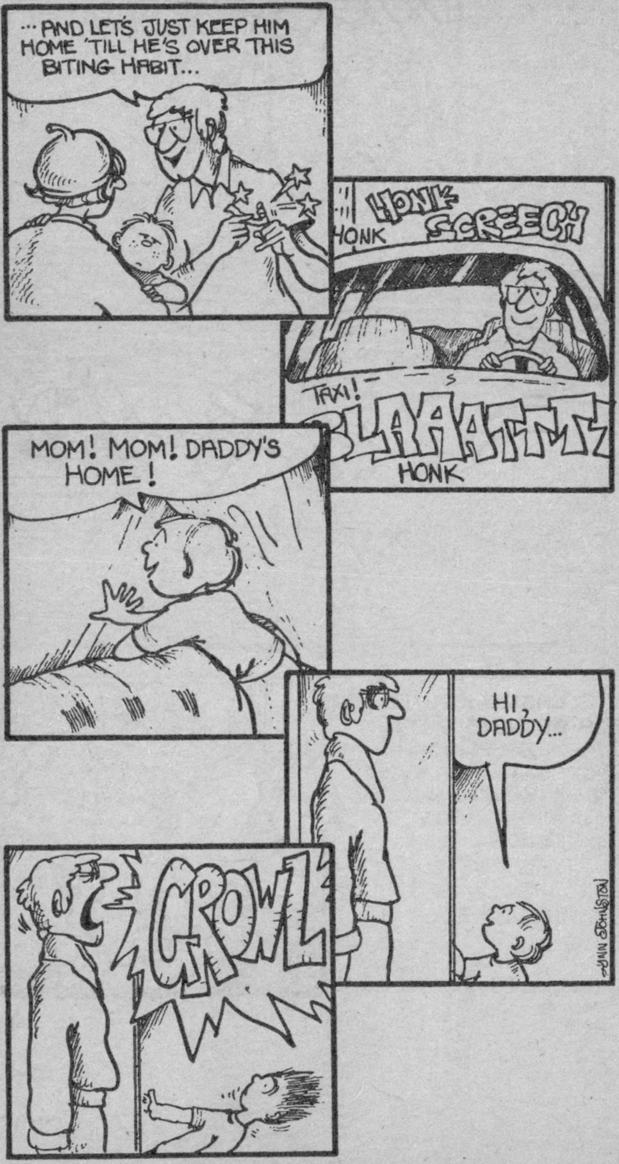
...AND LET'S JUST KEEP HIM HOME 'TILL HE'S OVER THIS BITING HABIT...
HONK
HONK
SCREECH
TAXI!
BLAAATT
HONK
MOM! MOM! DADDY'S HOME!
HI, DADDY...
LYNN JOHNSTON
GROWL

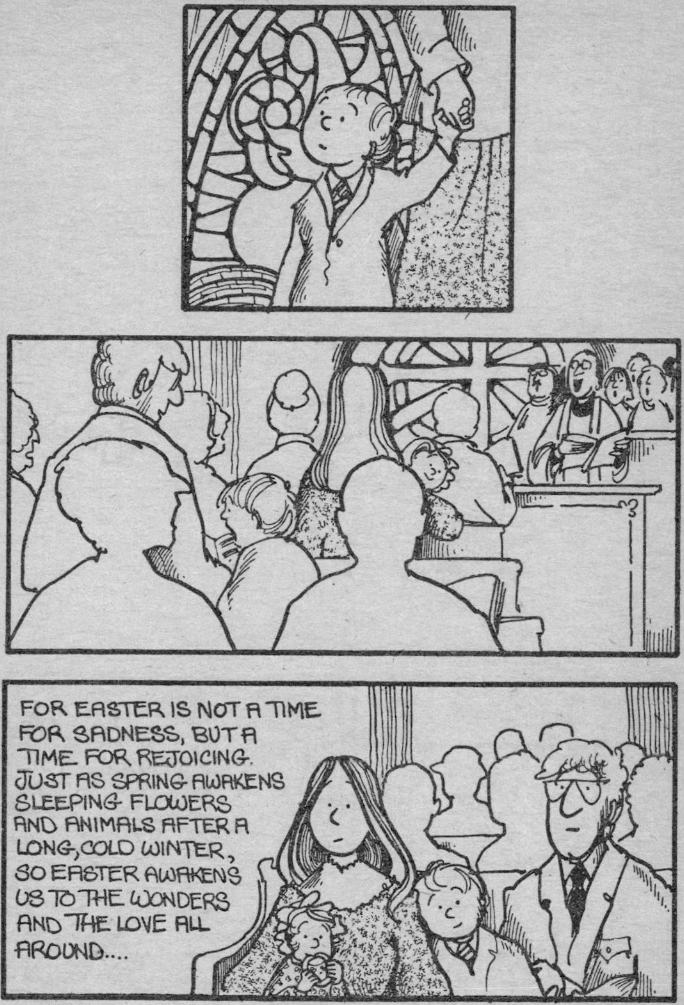
FOR EASTER IS NOT A TIME FOR SADNESS, BUT A TIME FOR REJOICING. JUST AS SPRING AWAKENS SLEEPING FLOWERS AND ANIMALS AFTER A LONG, COLD WINTER, SO EASTER AWAKENS US TO THE WONDERS AND THE LOVE ALL AROUND....

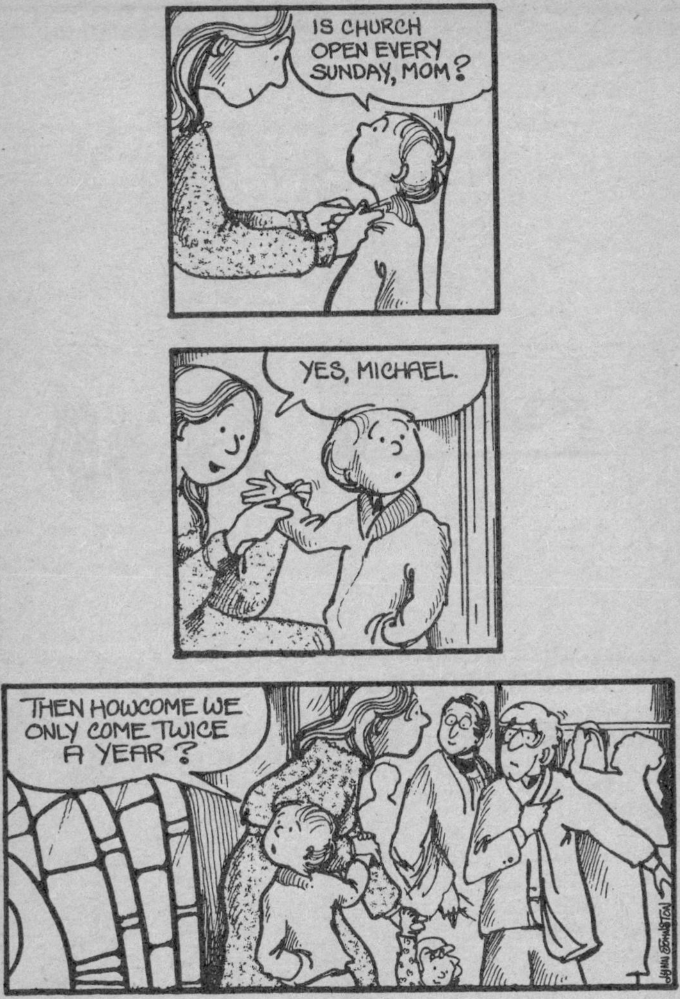
IS CHURCH OPEN EVERY SUNDAY, MOM?
YES, MICHAEL.
THEN HOWCOME WE ONLY COME TWICE A YEAR?

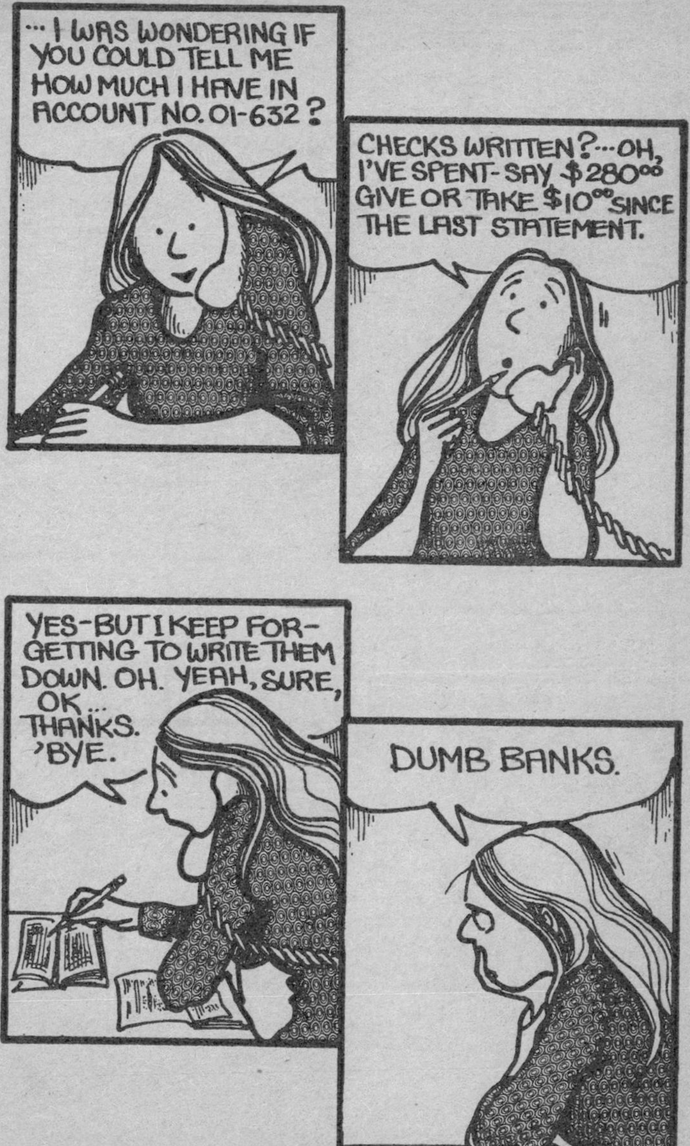
...I WAS WONDERING IF YOU COULD TELL ME HOW MUCH I HAVE IN ACCOUNT NO. 01-632?
CHECKS WRITTEN?...OH, I'VE SPENT- SAY $280.00 GIVE OR TAKE $10.00 SINCE THE LAST STATEMENT.
YES-BUT I KEEP FORGETTING TO WRITE THEM DOWN. OH. YEAH, SURE, OK... THANKS. 'BYE.
DUMB BANKS.

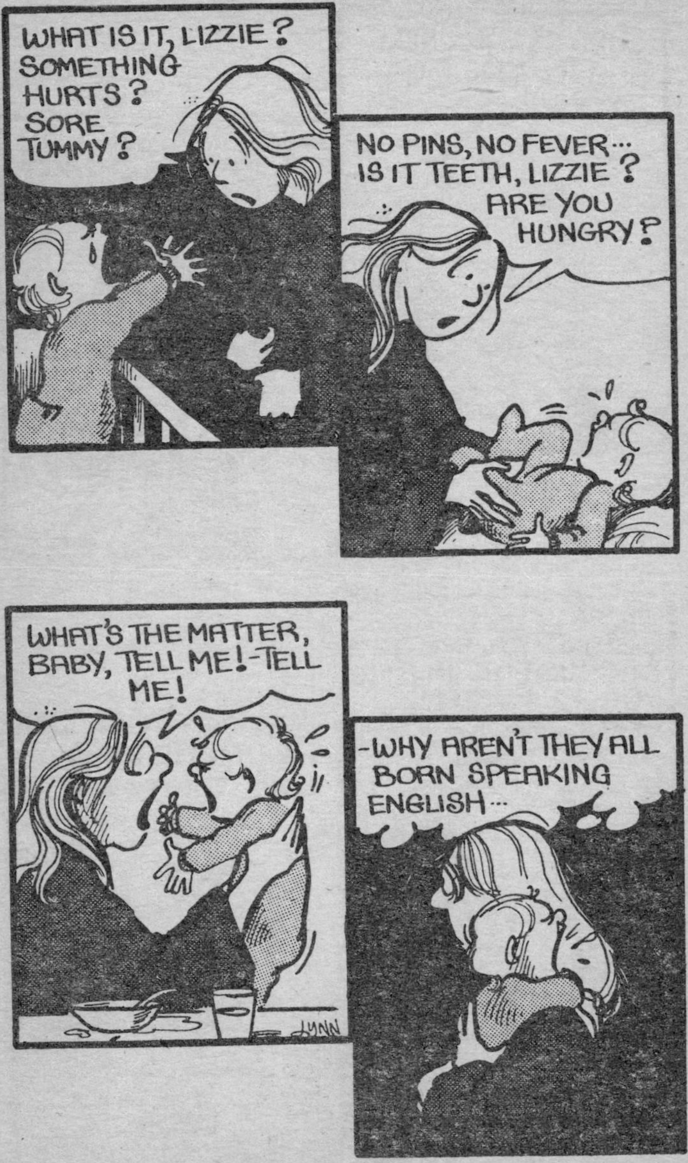
WHAT IS IT, LIZZIE? SOMETHING HURTS? SORE TUMMY?
NO PINS, NO FEVER... IS IT TEETH, LIZZIE? ARE YOU HUNGRY?
WHAT'S THE MATTER, BABY, TELL ME!-TELL ME!
LYNN
-WHY AREN'T THEY ALL BORN SPEAKING ENGLISH...

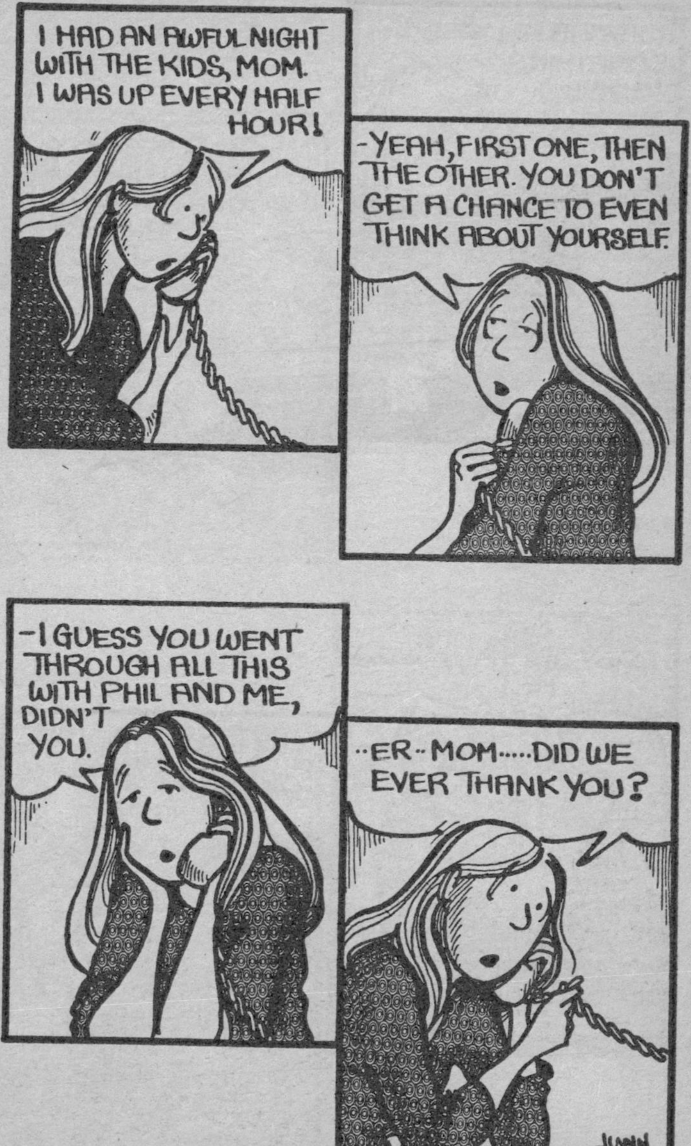
I HAD AN AWFUL NIGHT WITH THE KIDS, MOM. I WAS UP EVERY HALF HOUR!
-YEAH, FIRST ONE, THEN THE OTHER. YOU DON'T GET A CHANCE TO EVEN THINK ABOUT YOURSELF.
-I GUESS YOU WENT THROUGH ALL THIS WITH PHIL AND ME, DIDN'T YOU.
..ER..MOM.....DID WE EVER THANK YOU?
LYNN

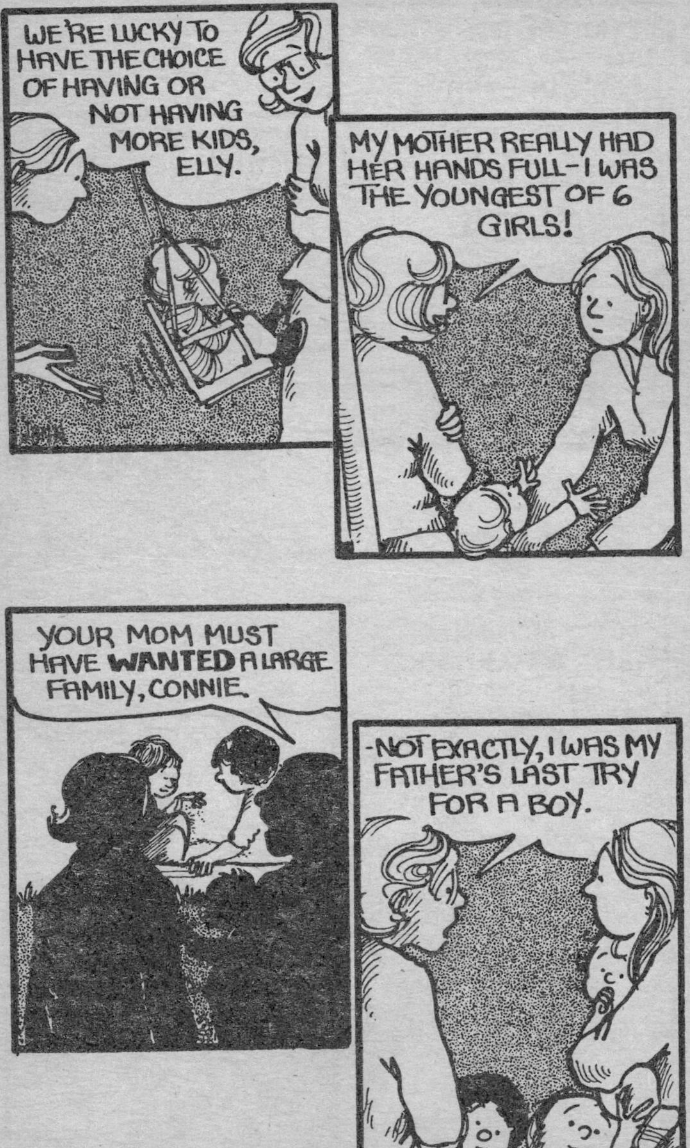
WE'RE LUCKY TO HAVE THE CHOICE OF HAVING OR NOT HAVING MORE KIDS, ELLY.
MY MOTHER REALLY HAD HER HANDS FULL-I WAS THE YOUNGEST OF 6 GIRLS!
YOUR MOM MUST HAVE **WANTED** A LARGE FAMILY, CONNIE.
-NOT EXACTLY, I WAS MY FATHER'S LAST TRY FOR A BOY.

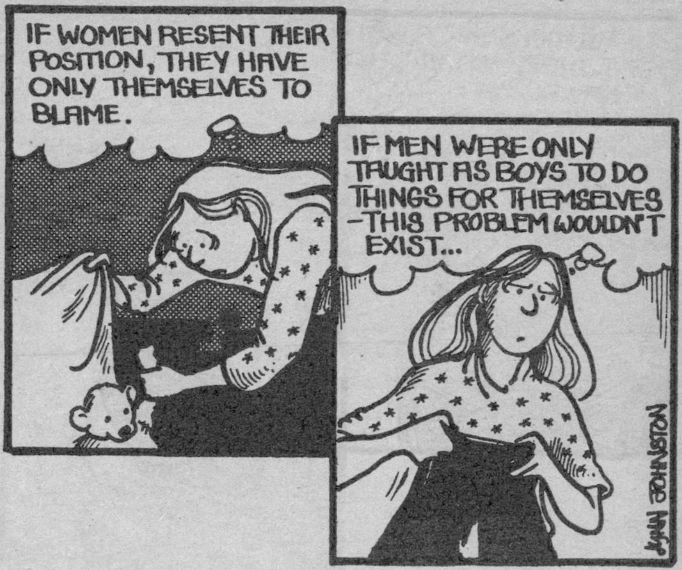
IF WOMEN RESENT THEIR POSITION, THEY HAVE ONLY THEMSELVES TO BLAME.
IF MEN WERE ONLY TAUGHT AS BOYS TO DO THINGS FOR THEMSELVES -THIS PROBLEM WOULDN'T EXIST...
LYNN JOHNSTON

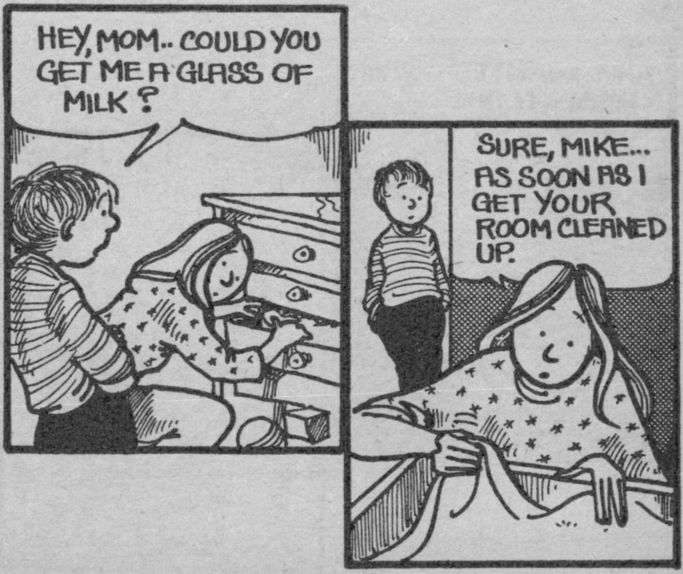
HEY, MOM.. COULD YOU GET ME A GLASS OF MILK?
SURE, MIKE... AS SOON AS I GET YOUR ROOM CLEANED UP.

I THINK I HAVE A CREDIT CARD···NO, WAIT, MAYBE I'VE GOT A CHECK...
CAN I GET A DOLLAR AND 80¢ WORTH OF REGULAR, PLEASE?
WHY DOES THIS THING ONLY RUN OUT OF GAS WHEN I'VE GOT IT!
LYNN

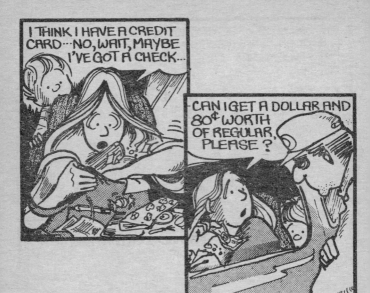

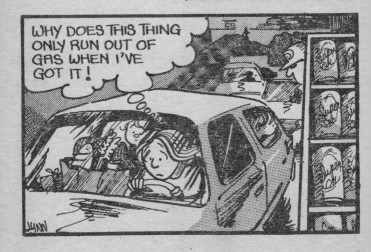

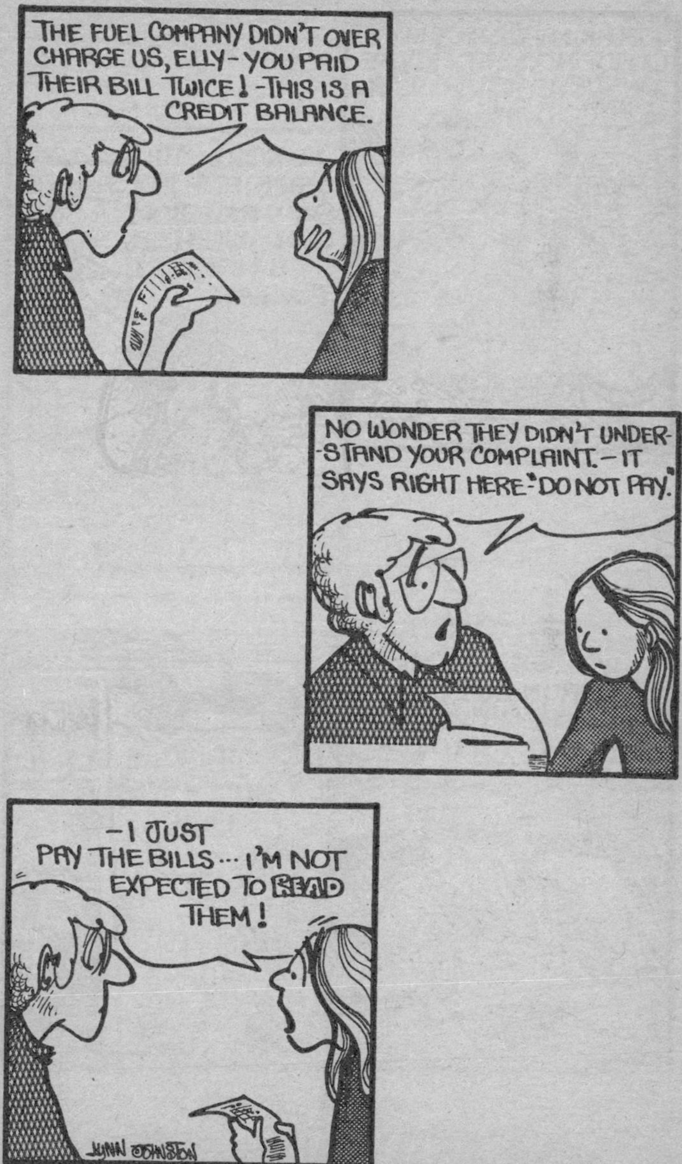
THE FUEL COMPANY DIDN'T OVER CHARGE US, ELLY - YOU PAID THEIR BILL TWICE! -THIS IS A CREDIT BALANCE.
NO WONDER THEY DIDN'T UNDER-STAND YOUR COMPLAINT. - IT SAYS RIGHT HERE: "DO NOT PAY."
-I JUST PAY THE BILLS... I'M NOT EXPECTED TO READ THEM!
LYNN JOHNSTON

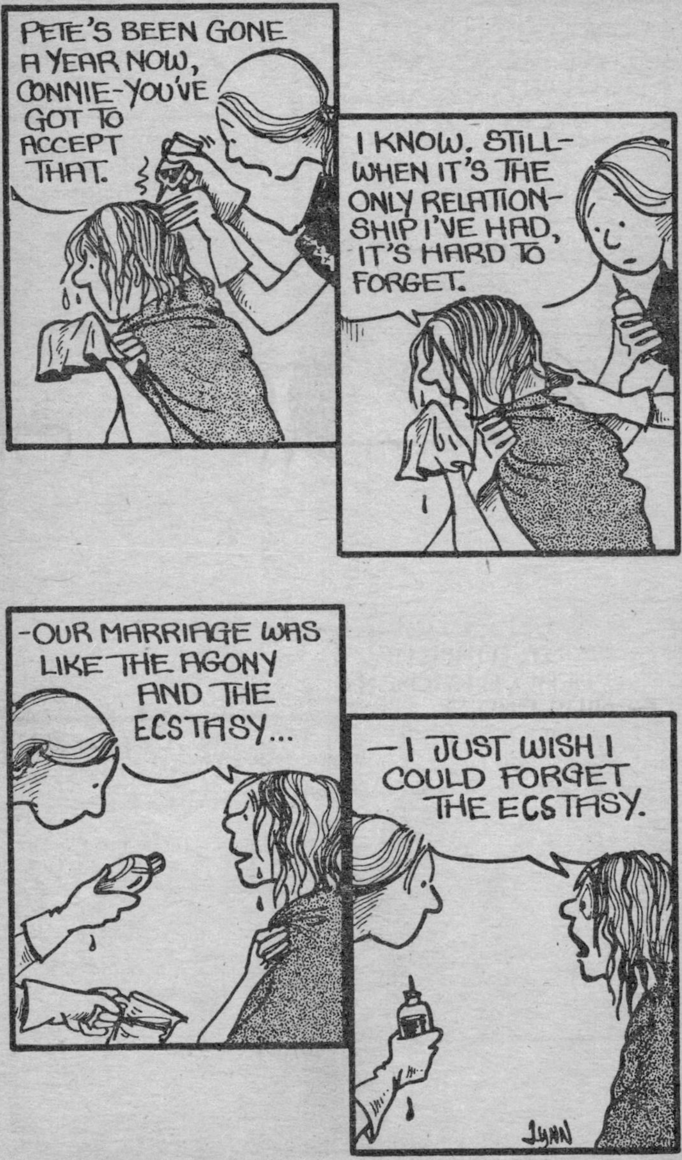
PETE'S BEEN GONE A YEAR NOW, CONNIE-YOU'VE GOT TO ACCEPT THAT.
I KNOW. STILL-WHEN IT'S THE ONLY RELATION-SHIP I'VE HAD, IT'S HARD TO FORGET.
-OUR MARRIAGE WAS LIKE THE AGONY AND THE ECSTASY...
—I JUST WISH I COULD FORGET THE ECSTASY.
LYNN

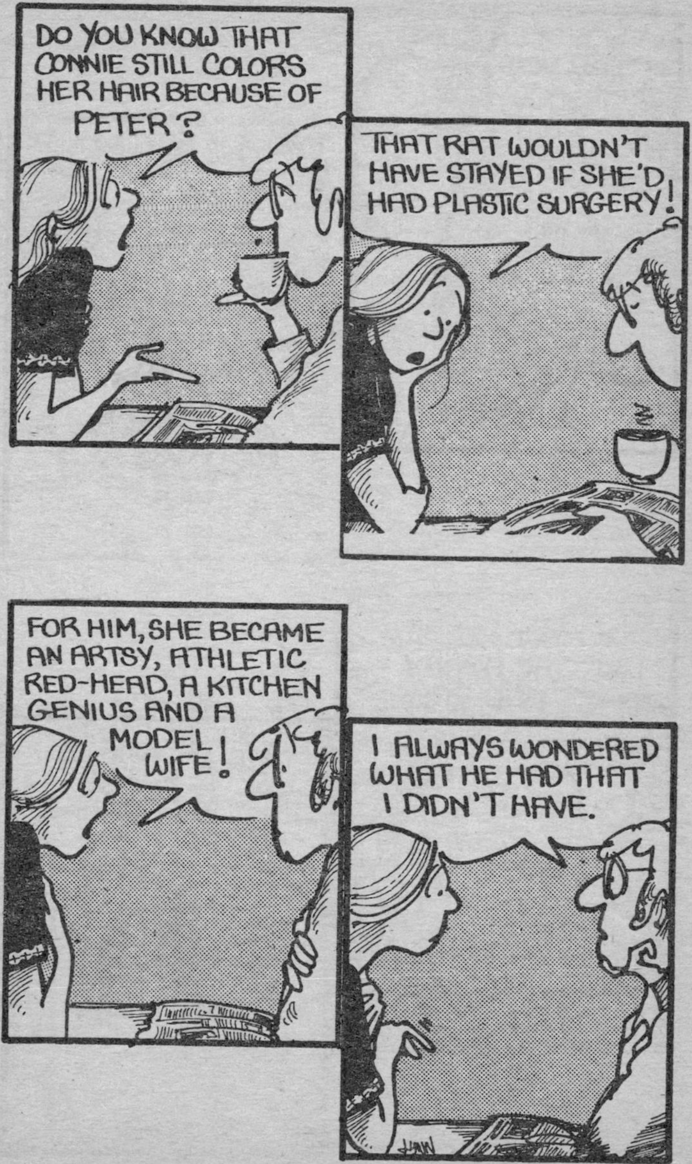
DO YOU KNOW THAT CONNIE STILL COLORS HER HAIR BECAUSE OF PETER?
THAT RAT WOULDN'T HAVE STAYED IF SHE'D HAD PLASTIC SURGERY!
FOR HIM, SHE BECAME AN ARTSY, ATHLETIC RED-HEAD, A KITCHEN GENIUS AND A MODEL WIFE!
I ALWAYS WONDERED WHAT HE HAD THAT I DIDN'T HAVE.

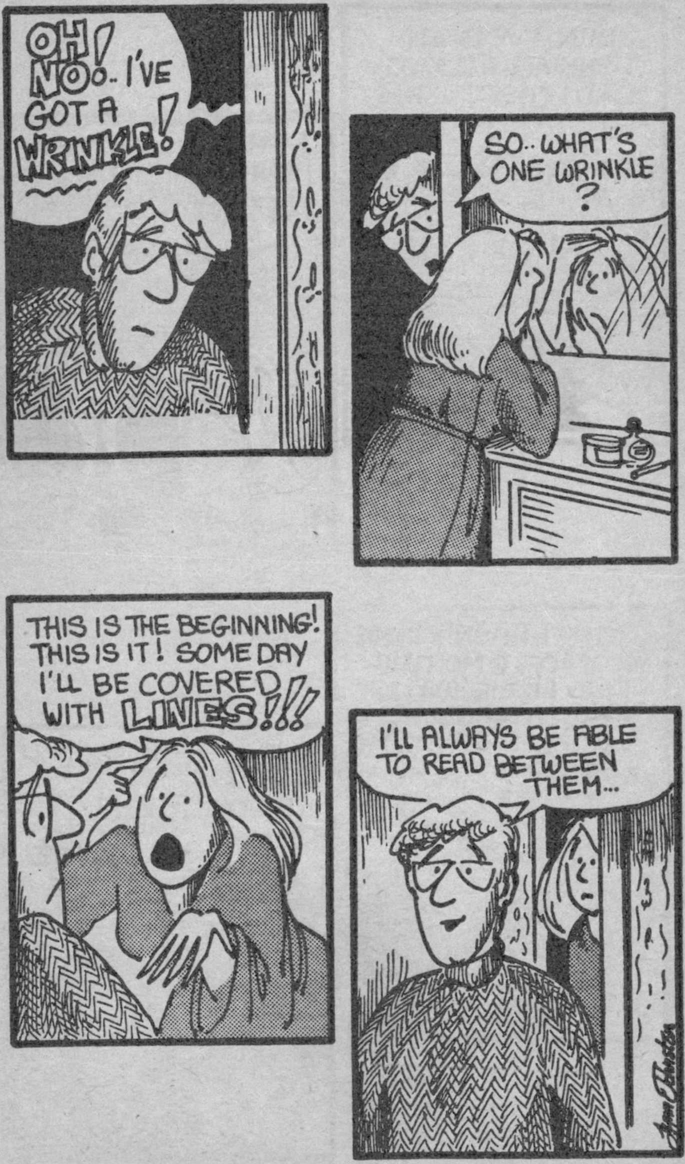
OH! NO!.. I'VE GOT A WRINKLE!
SO.. WHAT'S ONE WRINKLE?
THIS IS THE BEGINNING! THIS IS IT! SOME DAY I'LL BE COVERED WITH LINES!!!
I'LL ALWAYS BE ABLE TO READ BETWEEN THEM...

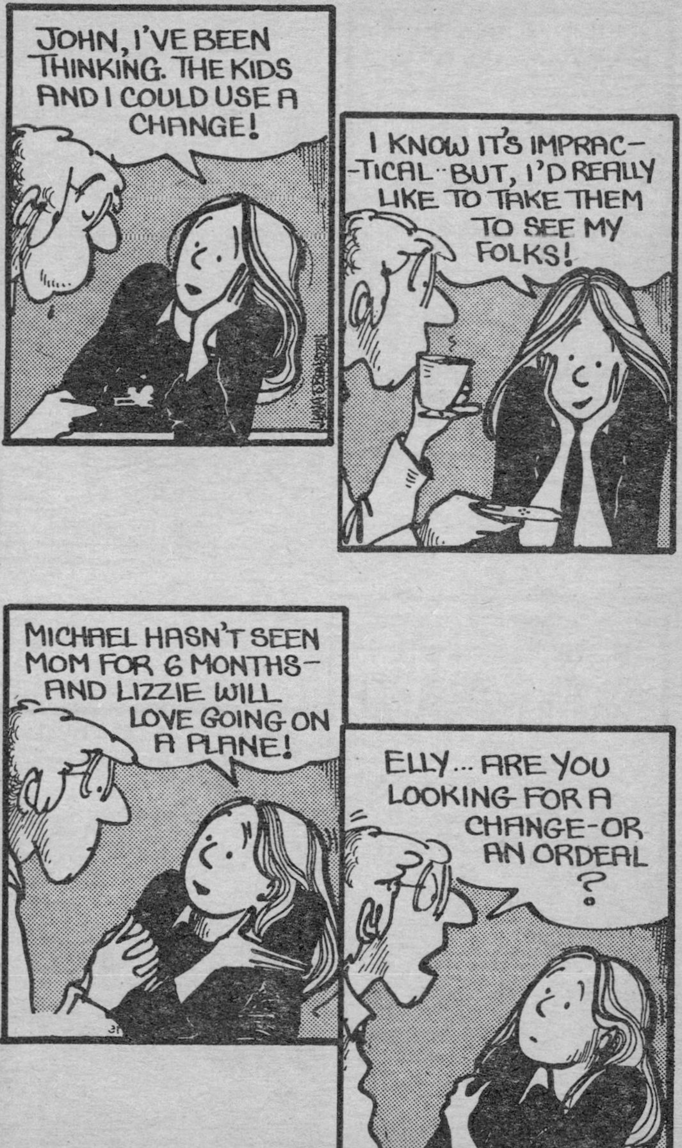
JOHN, I'VE BEEN THINKING. THE KIDS AND I COULD USE A CHANGE!
I KNOW IT'S IMPRAC--TICAL.. BUT, I'D REALLY LIKE TO TAKE THEM TO SEE MY FOLKS!
MICHAEL HASN'T SEEN MOM FOR 6 MONTHS-AND LIZZIE WILL LOVE GOING ON A PLANE!
ELLY... ARE YOU LOOKING FOR A CHANGE-OR AN ORDEAL?

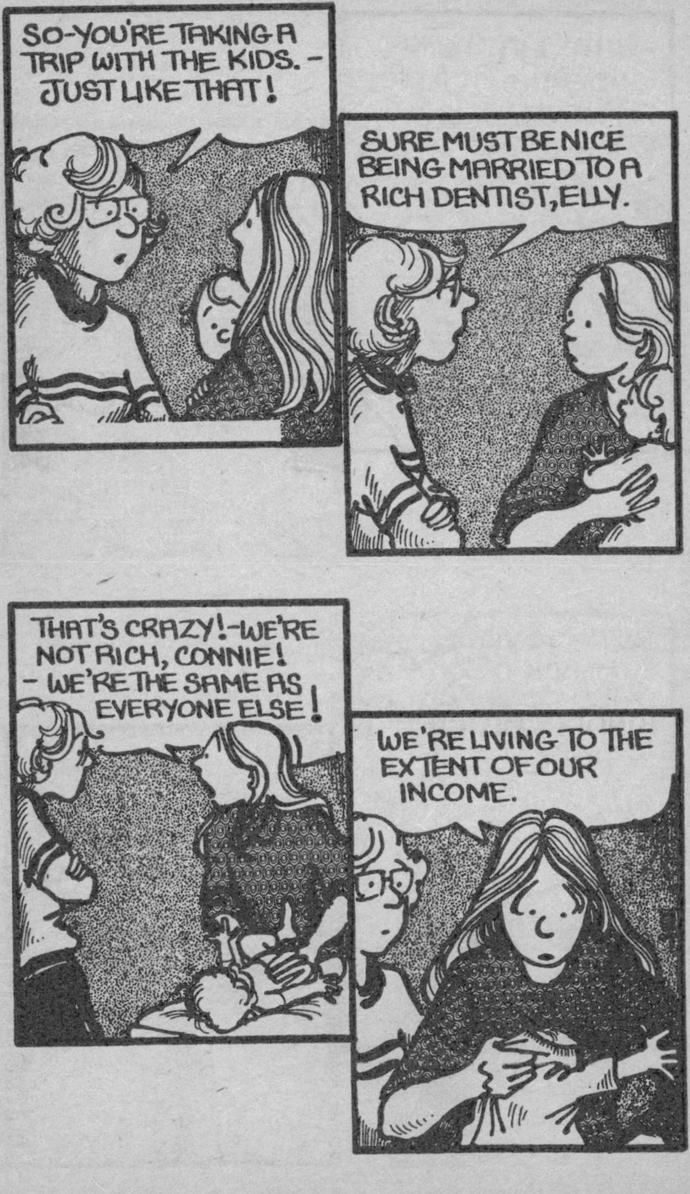
SO-YOU'RE TAKING A TRIP WITH THE KIDS. - JUST LIKE THAT!
SURE MUST BE NICE BEING MARRIED TO A RICH DENTIST, ELLY.
THAT'S CRAZY! - WE'RE NOT RICH, CONNIE! - WE'RE THE SAME AS EVERYONE ELSE!
WE'RE LIVING TO THE EXTENT OF OUR INCOME.

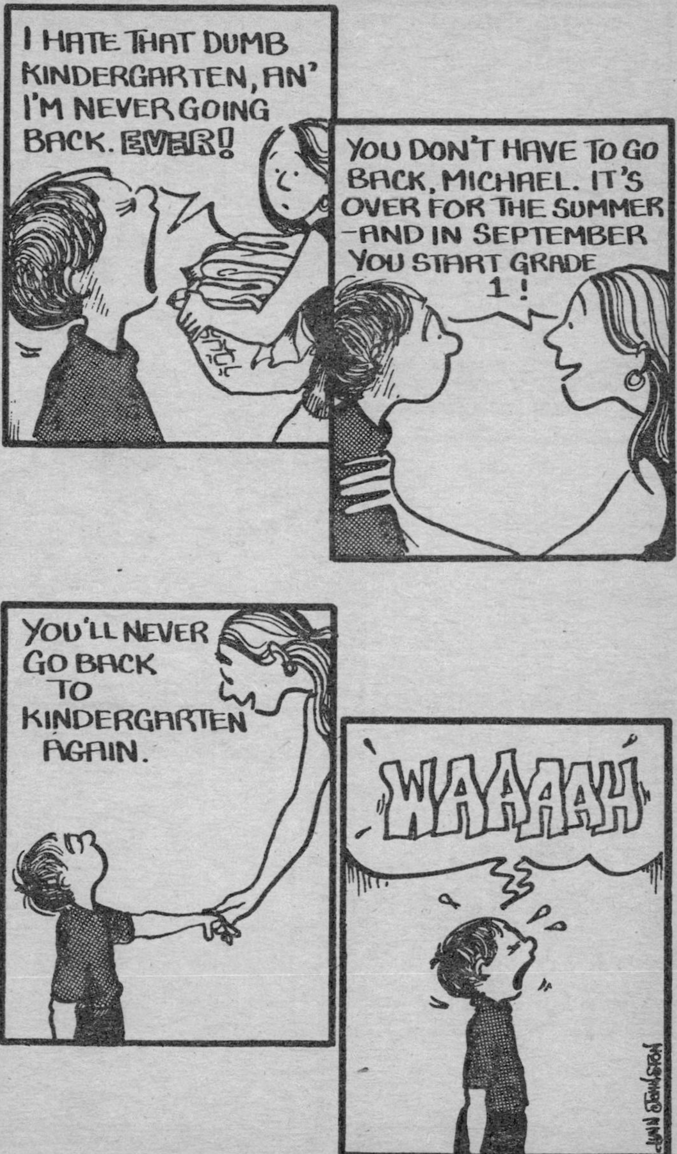
I HATE THAT DUMB KINDERGARTEN, AN' I'M NEVER GOING BACK. EVER!
YOU DON'T HAVE TO GO BACK, MICHAEL. IT'S OVER FOR THE SUMMER —AND IN SEPTEMBER YOU START GRADE 1!
YOU'LL NEVER GO BACK TO KINDERGARTEN AGAIN.
WAAAAH
LYNN JOHNSTON

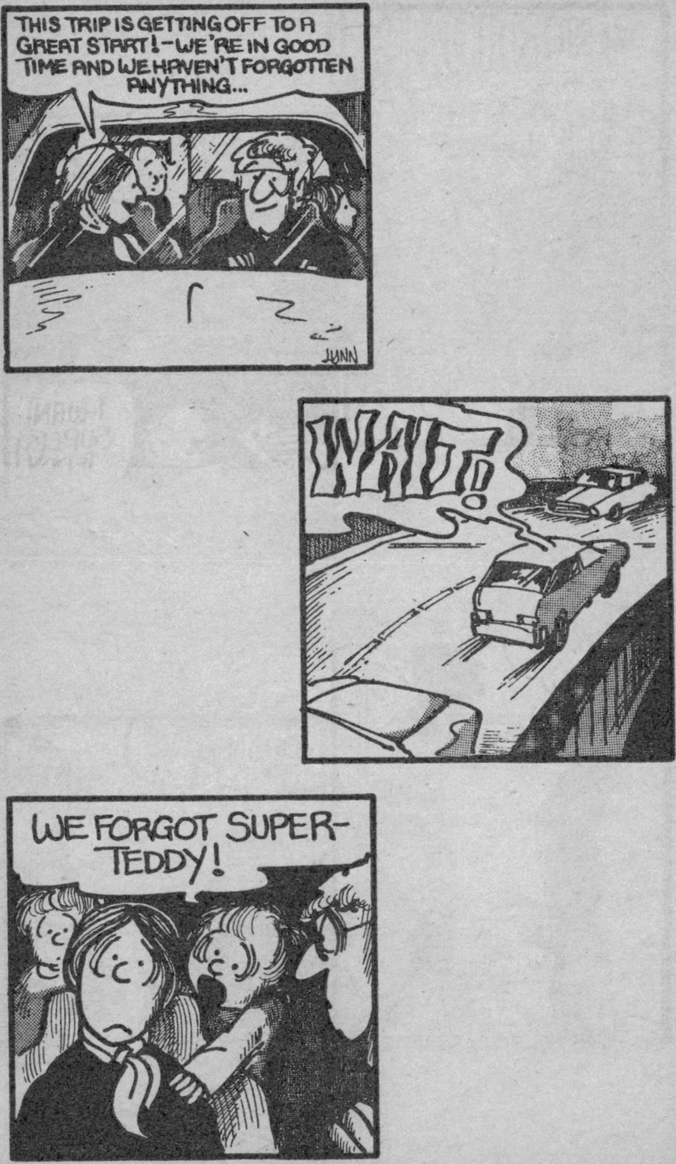
THIS TRIP IS GETTING OFF TO A GREAT START!-WE'RE IN GOOD TIME AND WE HAVEN'T FORGOTTEN ANYTHING...
LYNN
WAIT!
WE FORGOT SUPER-TEDDY!

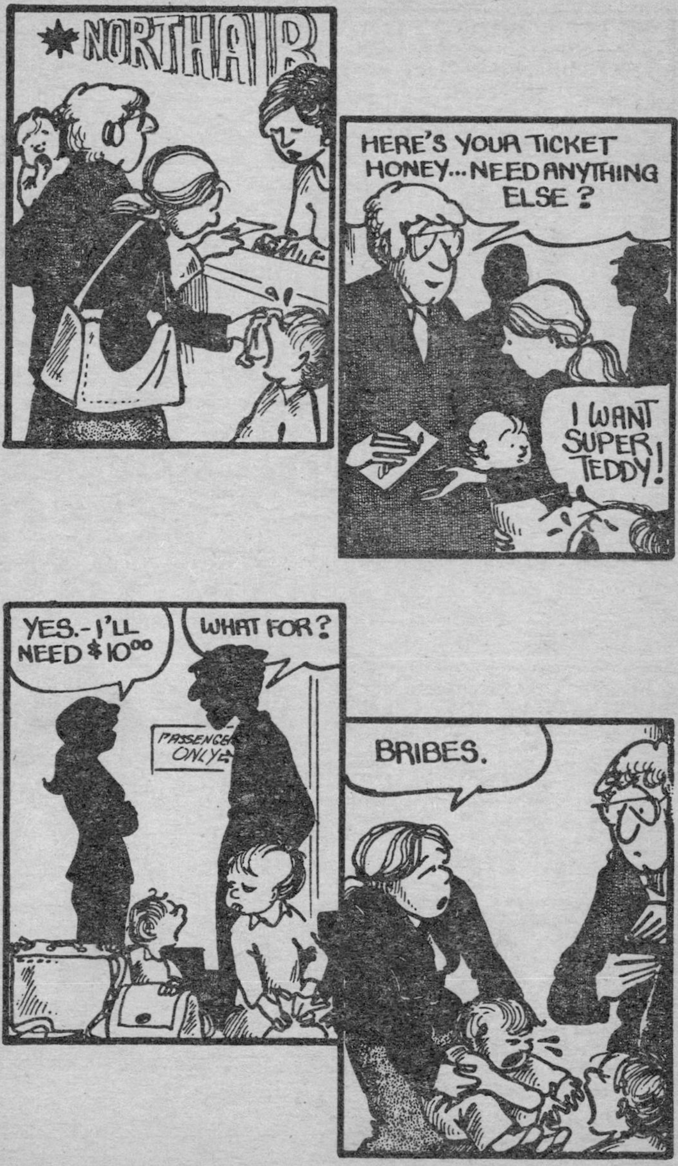
NORTHAIR
HERE'S YOUR TICKET HONEY... NEED ANYTHING ELSE ?
I WANT SUPER TEDDY!
YES.- I'LL NEED $10.00
WHAT FOR ?
PASSENGERS ONLY
BRIBES.

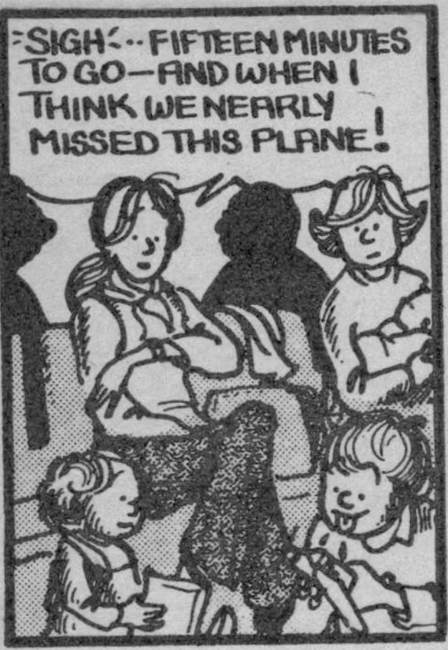
SIGH... FIFTEEN MINUTES TO GO—AND WHEN I THINK WE NEARLY MISSED THIS PLANE!

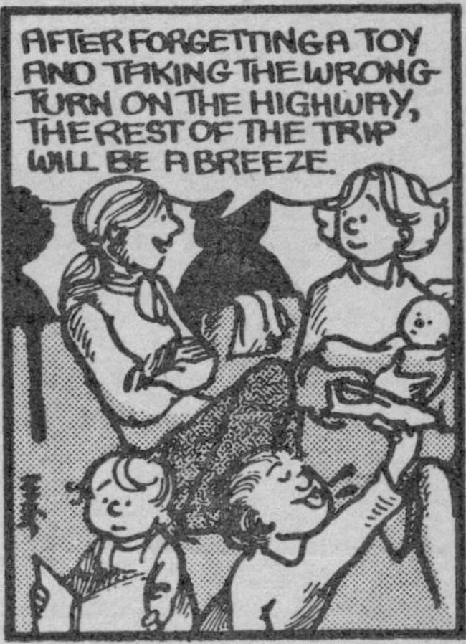
AFTER FORGETTING A TOY AND TAKING THE WRONG TURN ON THE HIGHWAY, THE REST OF THE TRIP WILL BE A BREEZE.

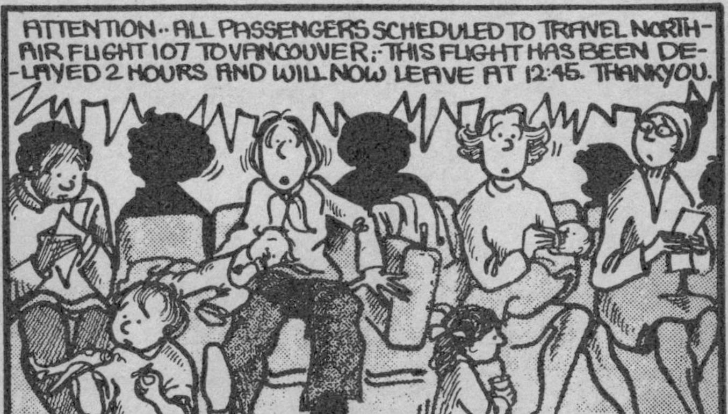
ATTENTION.. ALL PASSENGERS SCHEDULED TO TRAVEL NORTH-AIR FLIGHT 107 TO VANCOUVER;- THIS FLIGHT HAS BEEN DE-LAYED 2 HOURS AND WILL NOW LEAVE AT 12:45. THANKYOU.

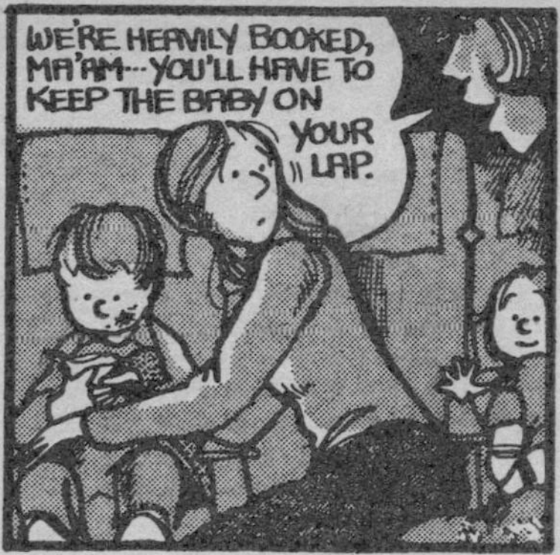
WE'RE HEAVILY BOOKED, MA'AM--- YOU'LL HAVE TO KEEP THE BABY ON YOUR LAP.

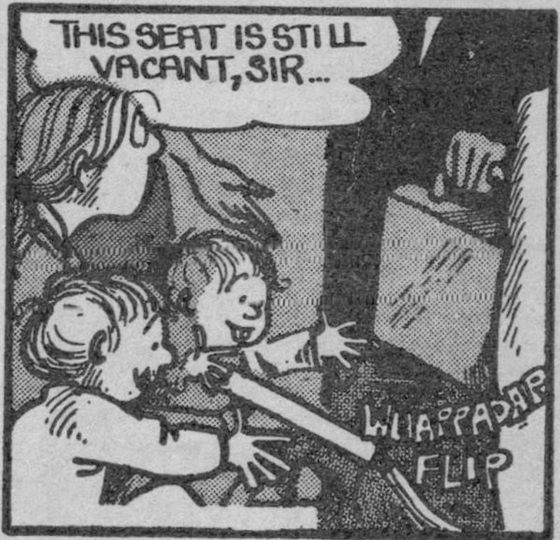
THIS SEAT IS STILL VACANT, SIR...
WHAPPADAP
FLIP

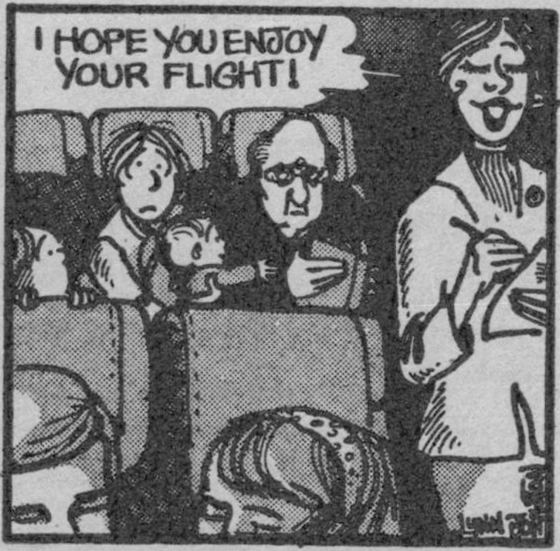
I HOPE YOU ENJOY YOUR FLIGHT!

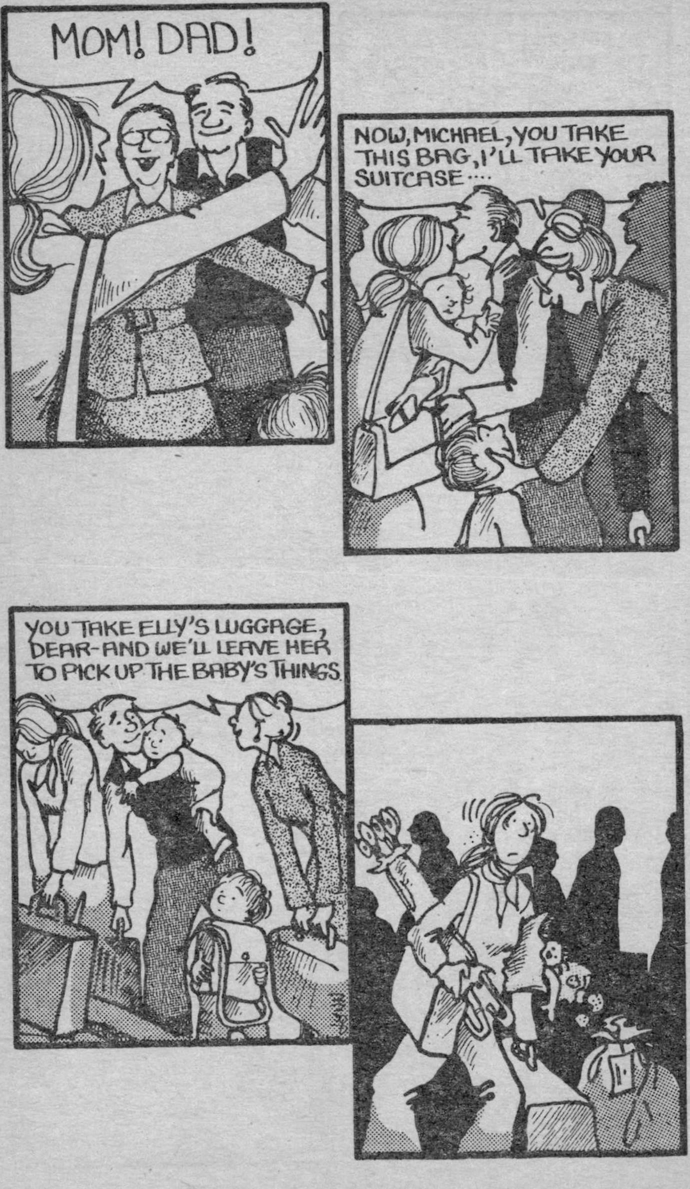
MOM! DAD!
NOW, MICHAEL, YOU TAKE THIS BAG, I'LL TAKE YOUR SUITCASE....
YOU TAKE ELLY'S LUGGAGE, DEAR-AND WE'LL LEAVE HER TO PICK UP THE BABY'S THINGS.

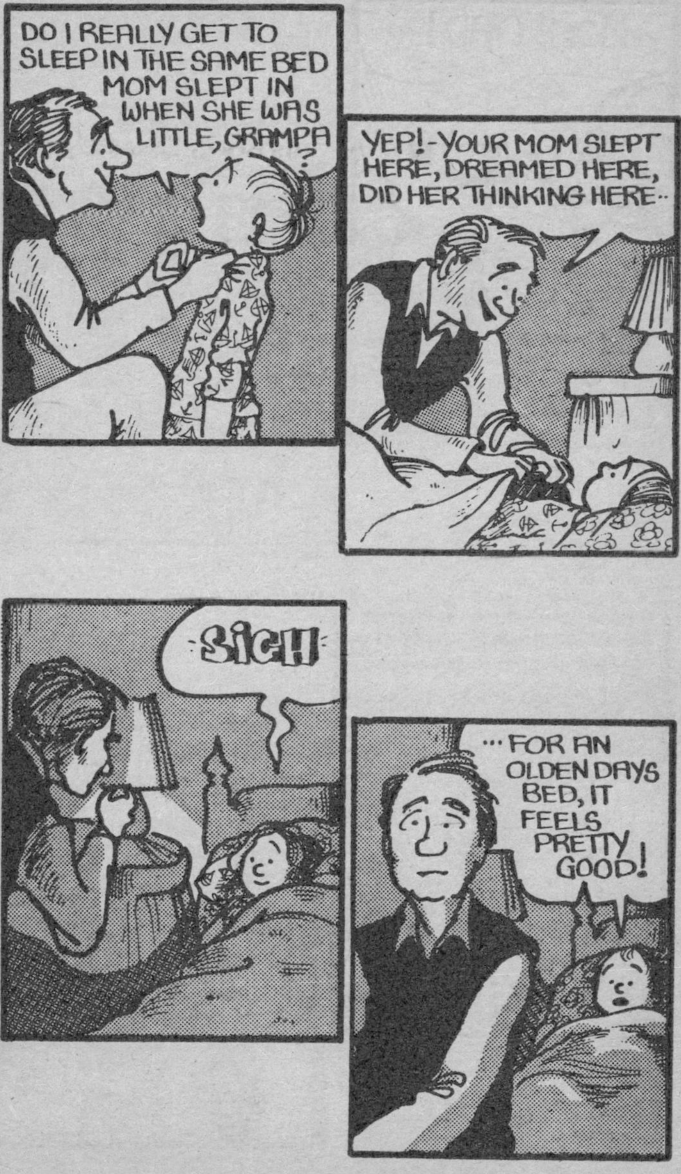
DO I REALLY GET TO SLEEP IN THE SAME BED MOM SLEPT IN WHEN SHE WAS LITTLE, GRAMPA?
YEP!-YOUR MOM SLEPT HERE, DREAMED HERE, DID HER THINKING HERE..
SIGH
...FOR AN OLDEN DAYS BED, IT FEELS PRETTY GOOD!

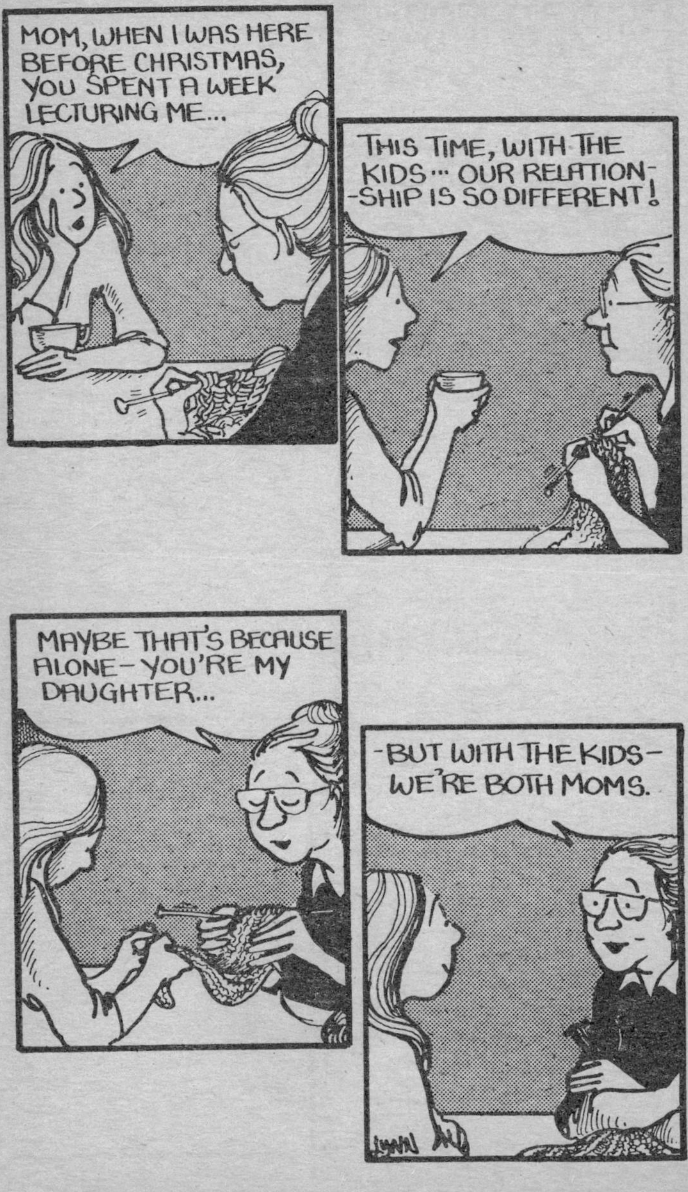
MOM, WHEN I WAS HERE BEFORE CHRISTMAS, YOU SPENT A WEEK LECTURING ME...
THIS TIME, WITH THE KIDS... OUR RELATION--SHIP IS SO DIFFERENT!
MAYBE THAT'S BECAUSE ALONE—YOU'RE MY DAUGHTER...
-BUT WITH THE KIDS-WE'RE BOTH MOMS.
LYNN

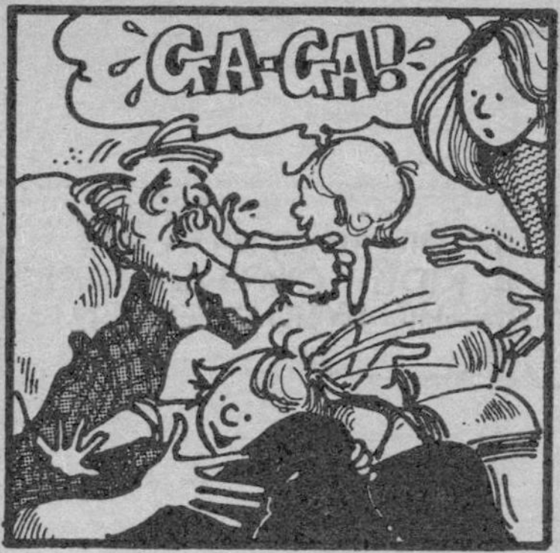
GA-GA!

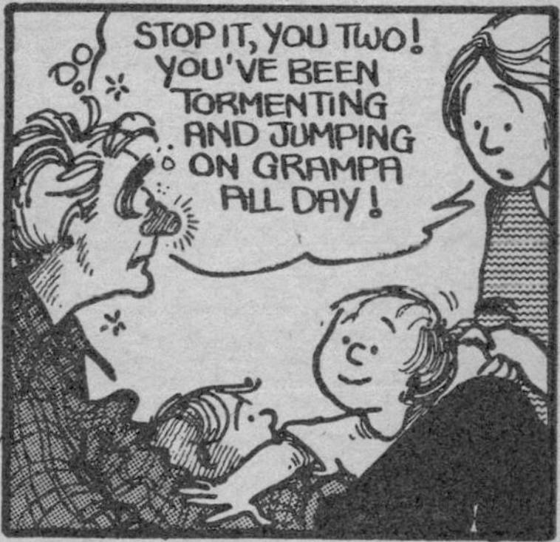
STOP IT, YOU TWO! YOU'VE BEEN TORMENTING AND JUMPING ON GRAMPA ALL DAY!

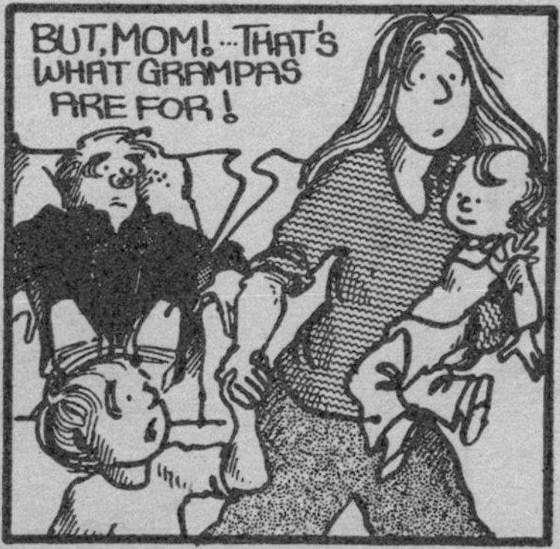
BUT, MOM! ...THAT'S WHAT GRAMPAS ARE FOR!

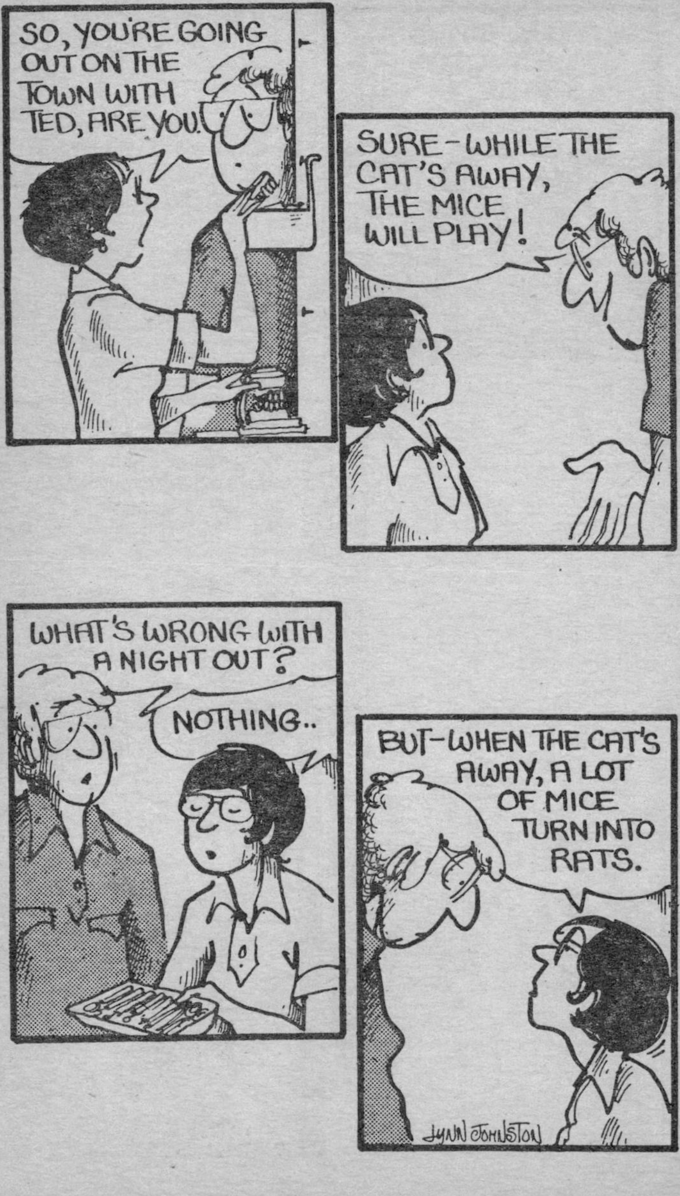
SO, YOU'RE GOING OUT ON THE TOWN WITH TED, ARE YOU.
SURE-WHILE THE CAT'S AWAY, THE MICE WILL PLAY!
WHAT'S WRONG WITH A NIGHT OUT?
NOTHING..
BUT-WHEN THE CAT'S AWAY, A LOT OF MICE TURN INTO RATS.
LYNN JOHNSTON

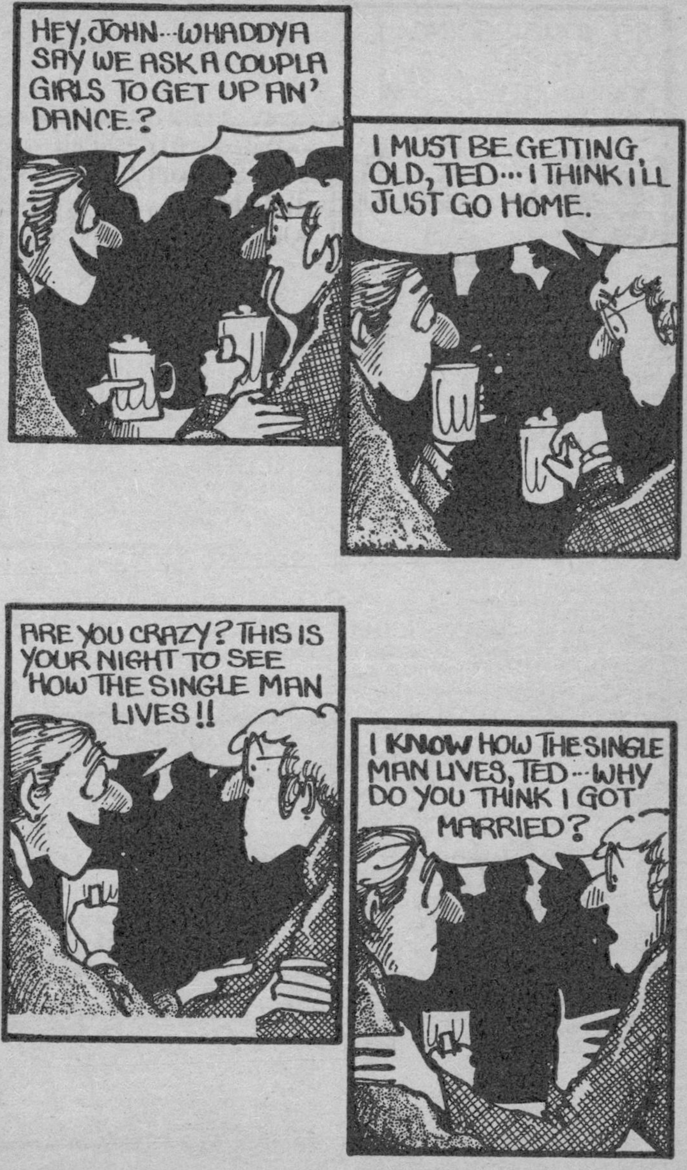
HEY, JOHN···WHADDYA SAY WE ASK A COUPLA GIRLS TO GET UP AN' DANCE?
I MUST BE GETTING OLD, TED··· I THINK I'LL JUST GO HOME.
ARE YOU CRAZY? THIS IS YOUR NIGHT TO SEE HOW THE SINGLE MAN LIVES!!
I KNOW HOW THE SINGLE MAN LIVES, TED···WHY DO YOU THINK I GOT MARRIED?

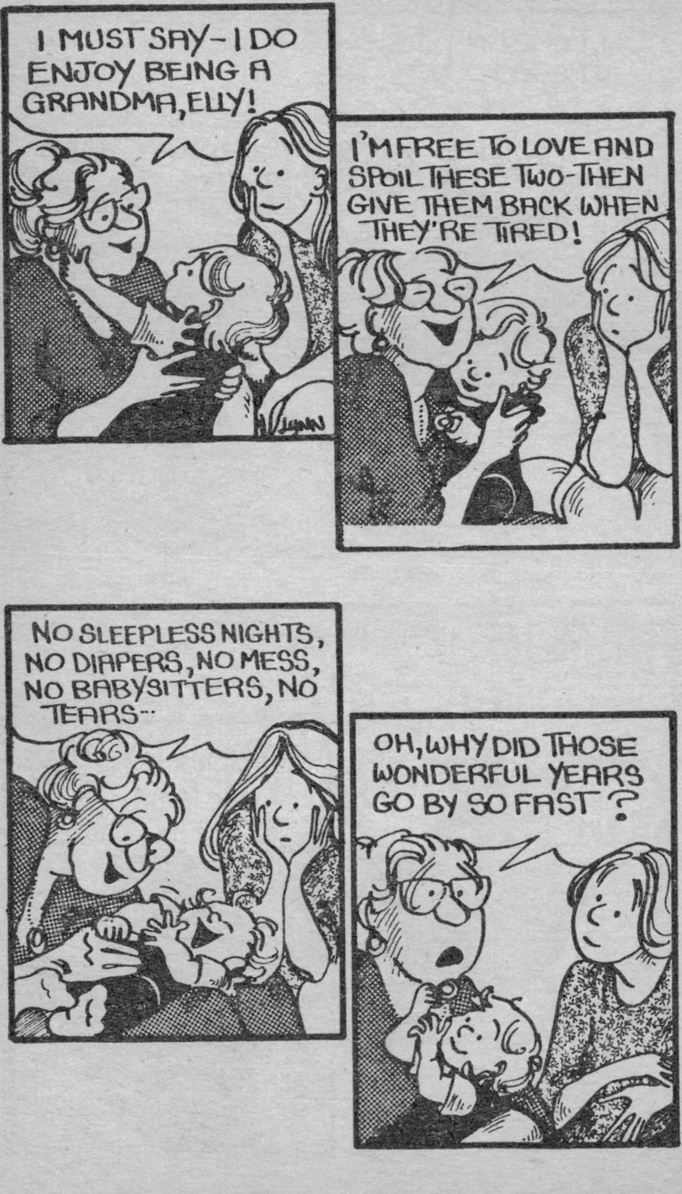
I MUST SAY-I DO ENJOY BEING A GRANDMA, ELLY!
I'M FREE TO LOVE AND SPOIL THESE TWO-THEN GIVE THEM BACK WHEN THEY'RE TIRED!
NO SLEEPLESS NIGHTS, NO DIAPERS, NO MESS, NO BABYSITTERS, NO TEARS...
OH, WHY DID THOSE WONDERFUL YEARS GO BY SO FAST?

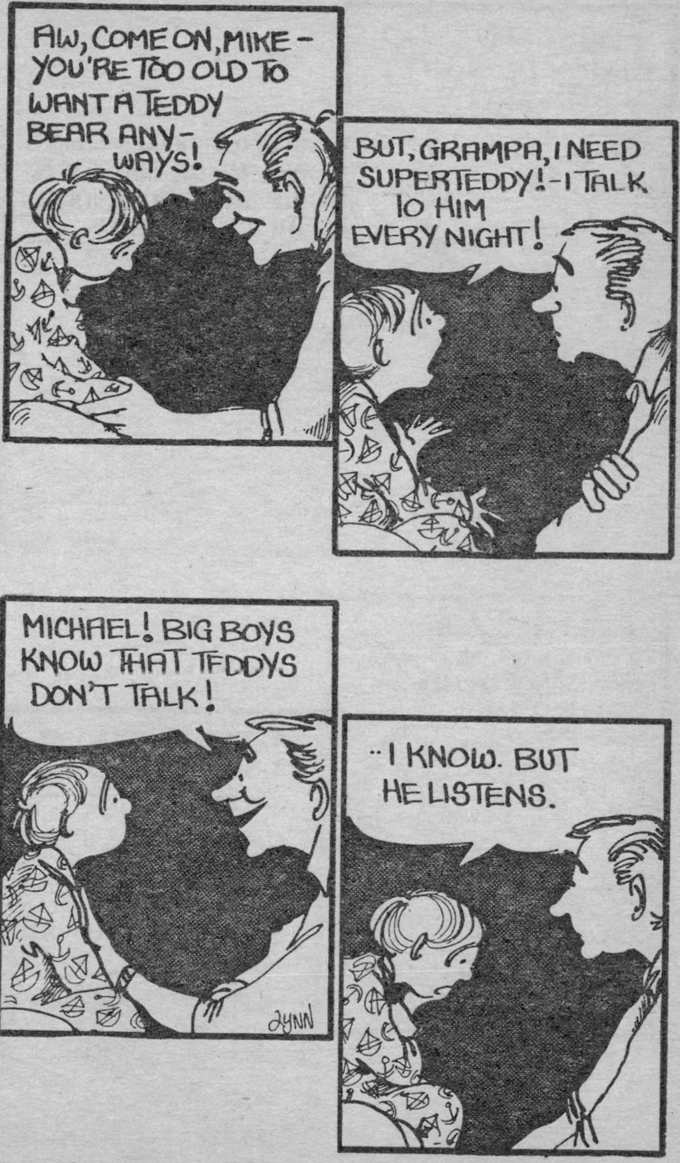
AW, COME ON, MIKE - YOU'RE TOO OLD TO WANT A TEDDY BEAR ANY-WAYS!
BUT, GRAMPA, I NEED SUPERTEDDY! - I TALK TO HIM EVERY NIGHT!
MICHAEL! BIG BOYS KNOW THAT TEDDYS DON'T TALK!
LYNN
..I KNOW. BUT HE LISTENS.

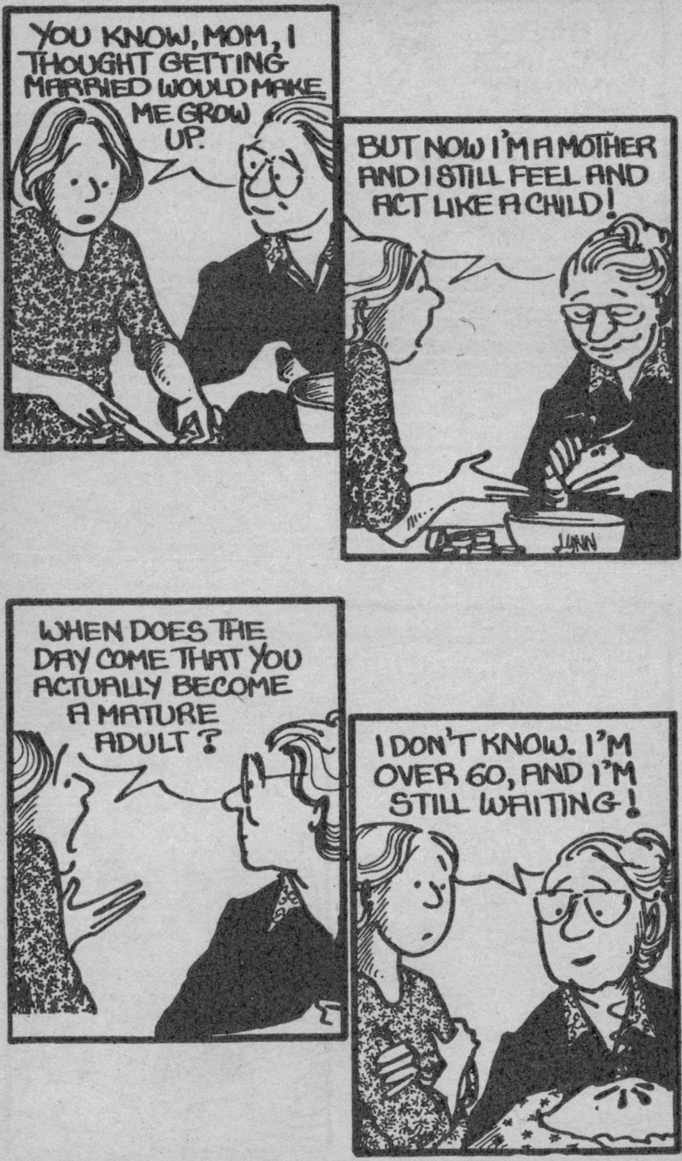
YOU KNOW, MOM, I THOUGHT GETTING MARRIED WOULD MAKE ME GROW UP.
BUT NOW I'M A MOTHER AND I STILL FEEL AND ACT LIKE A CHILD!
LYNN
WHEN DOES THE DAY COME THAT YOU ACTUALLY BECOME A MATURE ADULT?
I DON'T KNOW. I'M OVER 60, AND I'M STILL WAITING!

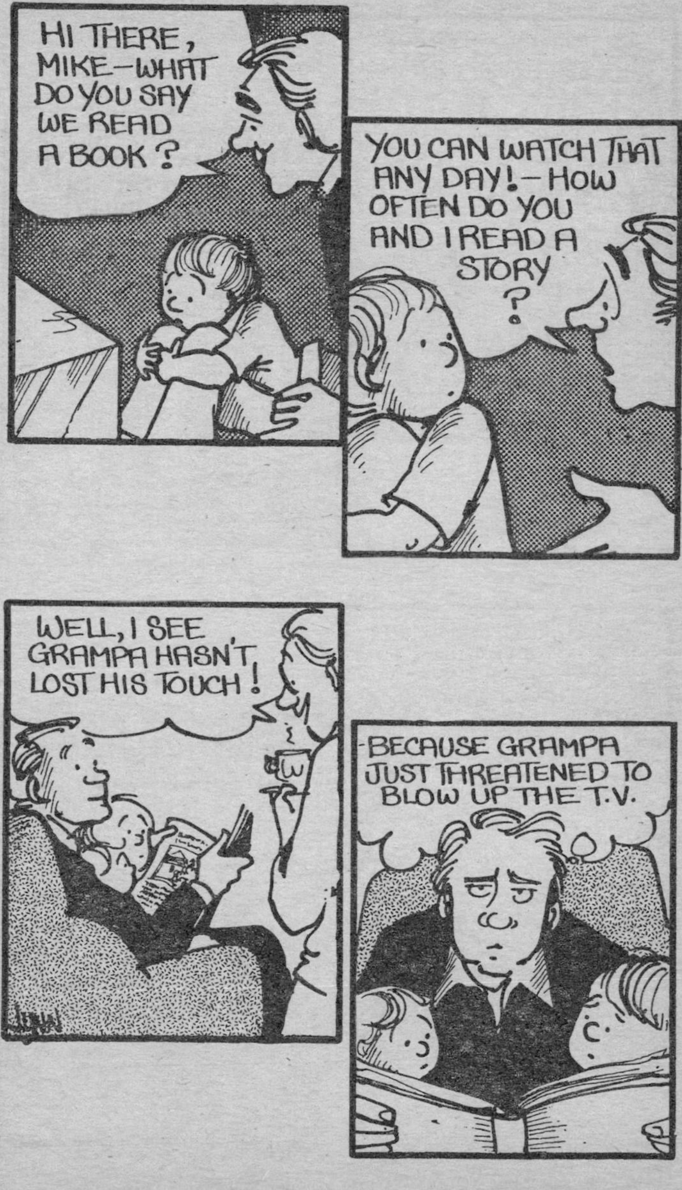
HI THERE, MIKE—WHAT DO YOU SAY WE READ A BOOK?
YOU CAN WATCH THAT ANY DAY!—HOW OFTEN DO YOU AND I READ A STORY?
WELL, I SEE GRAMPA HASN'T LOST HIS TOUCH!
-BECAUSE GRAMPA JUST THREATENED TO BLOW UP THE T.V.

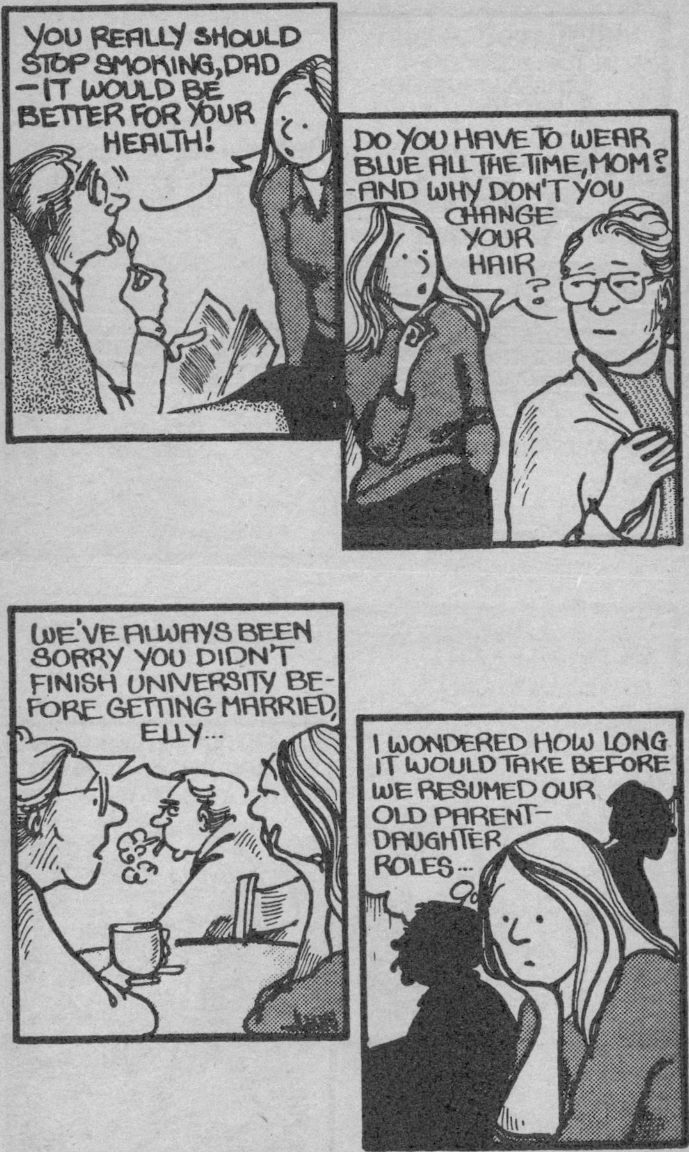

YOU REALLY SHOULD STOP SMOKING, DAD —IT WOULD BE BETTER FOR YOUR HEALTH!
DO YOU HAVE TO WEAR BLUE ALL THE TIME, MOM? -AND WHY DON'T YOU CHANGE YOUR HAIR?
WE'VE ALWAYS BEEN SORRY YOU DIDN'T FINISH UNIVERSITY BEFORE GETTING MARRIED, ELLY...
I WONDERED HOW LONG IT WOULD TAKE BEFORE WE RESUMED OUR OLD PARENT-DAUGHTER ROLES...

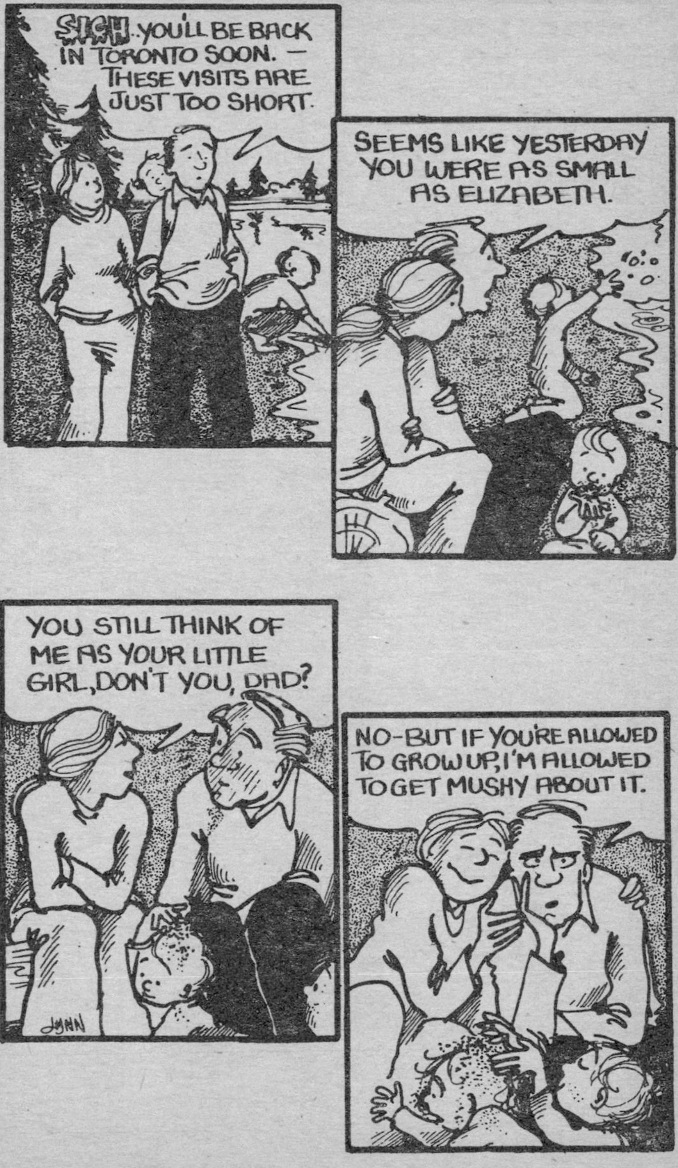
SIGH..YOU'LL BE BACK IN TORONTO SOON. — THESE VISITS ARE JUST TOO SHORT.
SEEMS LIKE YESTERDAY YOU WERE AS SMALL AS ELIZABETH.
YOU STILL THINK OF ME AS YOUR LITTLE GIRL, DON'T YOU, DAD?
NO-BUT IF YOU'RE ALLOWED TO GROW UP, I'M ALLOWED TO GET MUSHY ABOUT IT.
LYNN

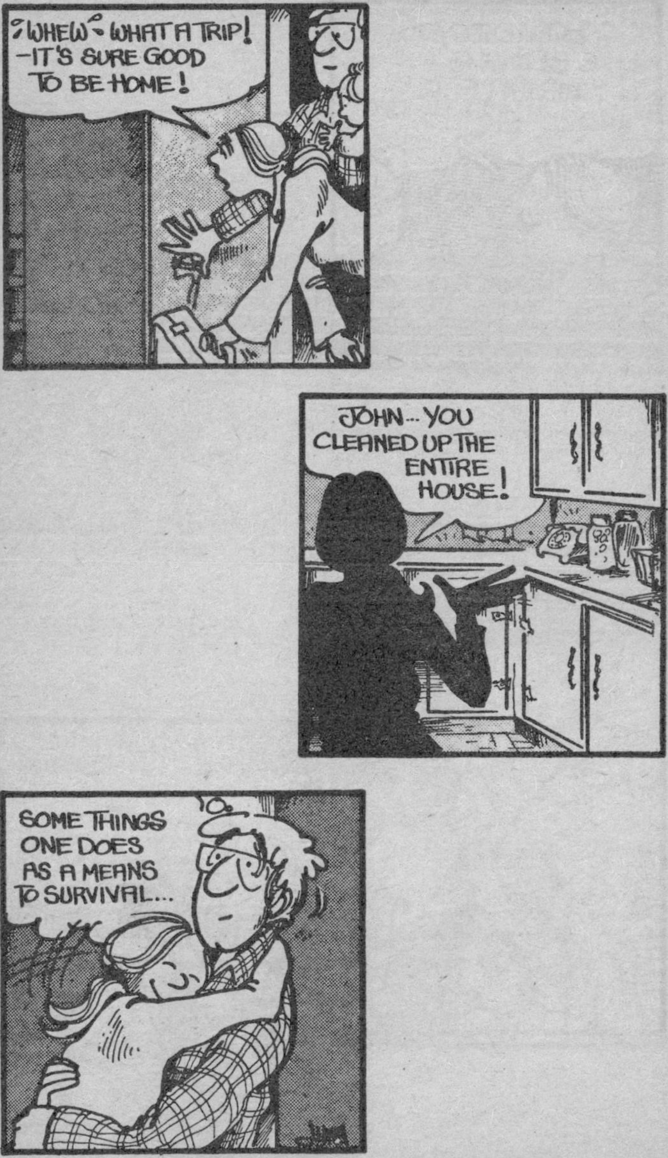
WHEW - WHAT A TRIP! -IT'S SURE GOOD TO BE HOME!
JOHN... YOU CLEANED UP THE ENTIRE HOUSE!
SOME THINGS ONE DOES AS A MEANS TO SURVIVAL...

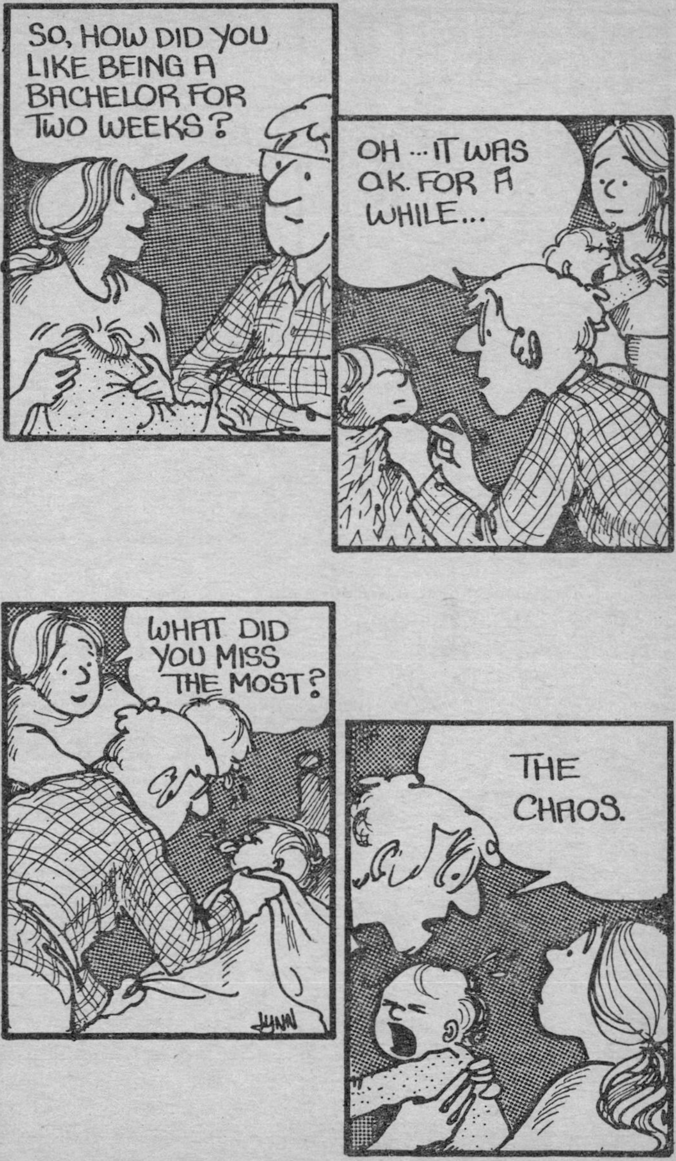
SO, HOW DID YOU LIKE BEING A BACHELOR FOR TWO WEEKS?
OH ... IT WAS O.K. FOR A WHILE...
WHAT DID YOU MISS THE MOST?
THE CHAOS.
LYNN

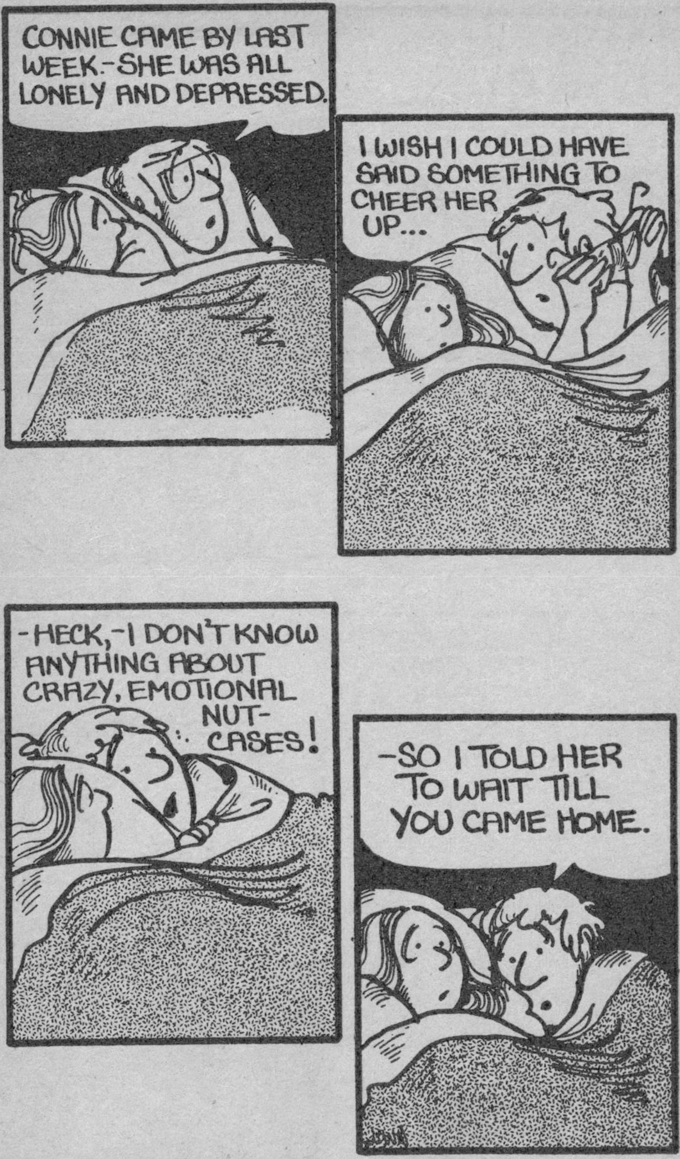
CONNIE CAME BY LAST WEEK.-SHE WAS ALL LONELY AND DEPRESSED.
I WISH I COULD HAVE SAID SOMETHING TO CHEER HER UP...
-HECK,-I DON'T KNOW ANYTHING ABOUT CRAZY, EMOTIONAL NUT-CASES!
-SO I TOLD HER TO WAIT TILL YOU CAME HOME.

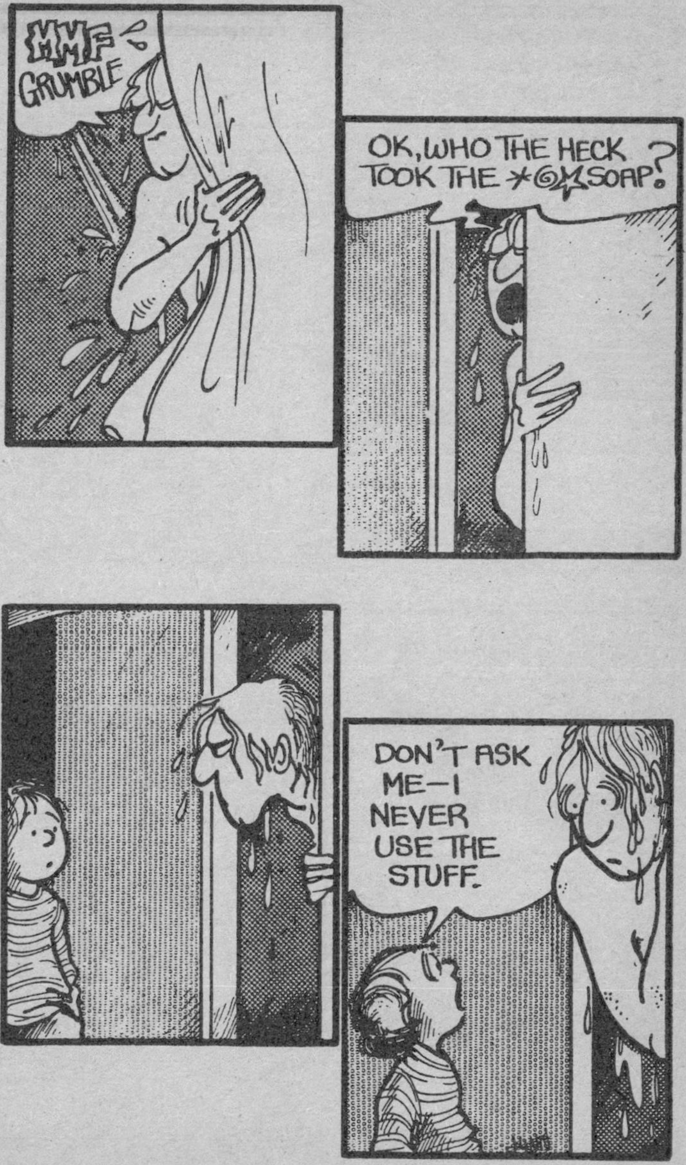
MMF GRUMBLE
OK, WHO THE HECK TOOK THE *@* SOAP?
DON'T ASK ME—I NEVER USE THE STUFF.

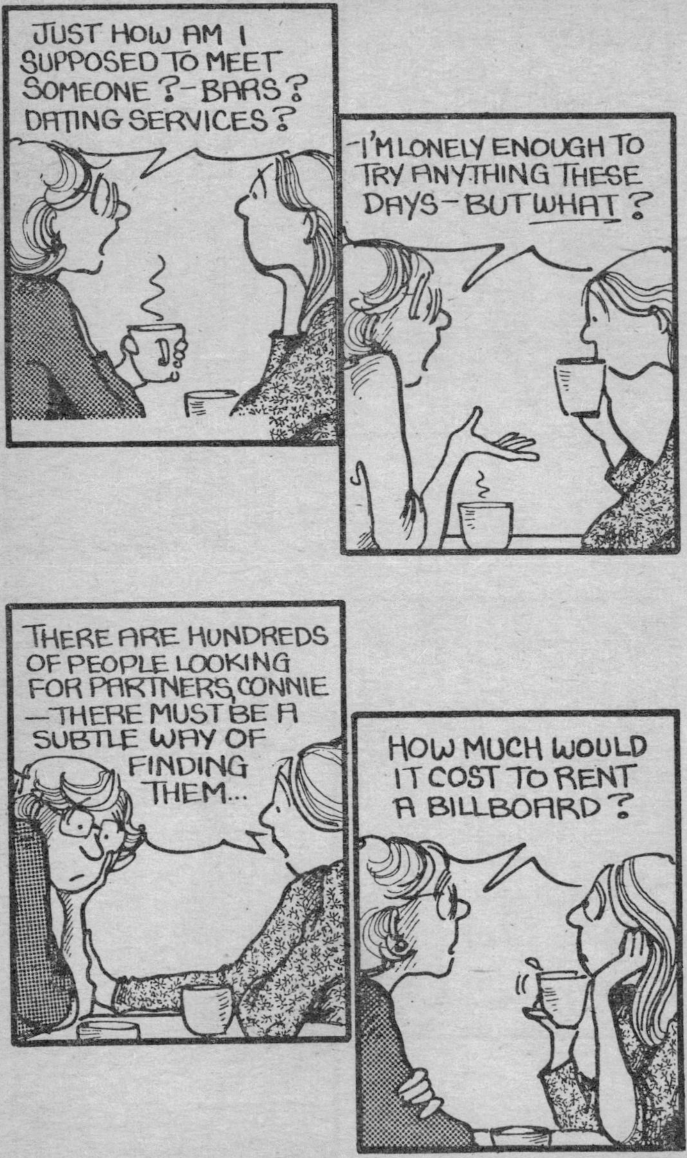
JUST HOW AM I SUPPOSED TO MEET SOMEONE?-BARS? DATING SERVICES?
-I'M LONELY ENOUGH TO TRY ANYTHING THESE DAYS-BUT WHAT?
THERE ARE HUNDREDS OF PEOPLE LOOKING FOR PARTNERS, CONNIE —THERE MUST BE A SUBTLE WAY OF FINDING THEM...
HOW MUCH WOULD IT COST TO RENT A BILLBOARD?

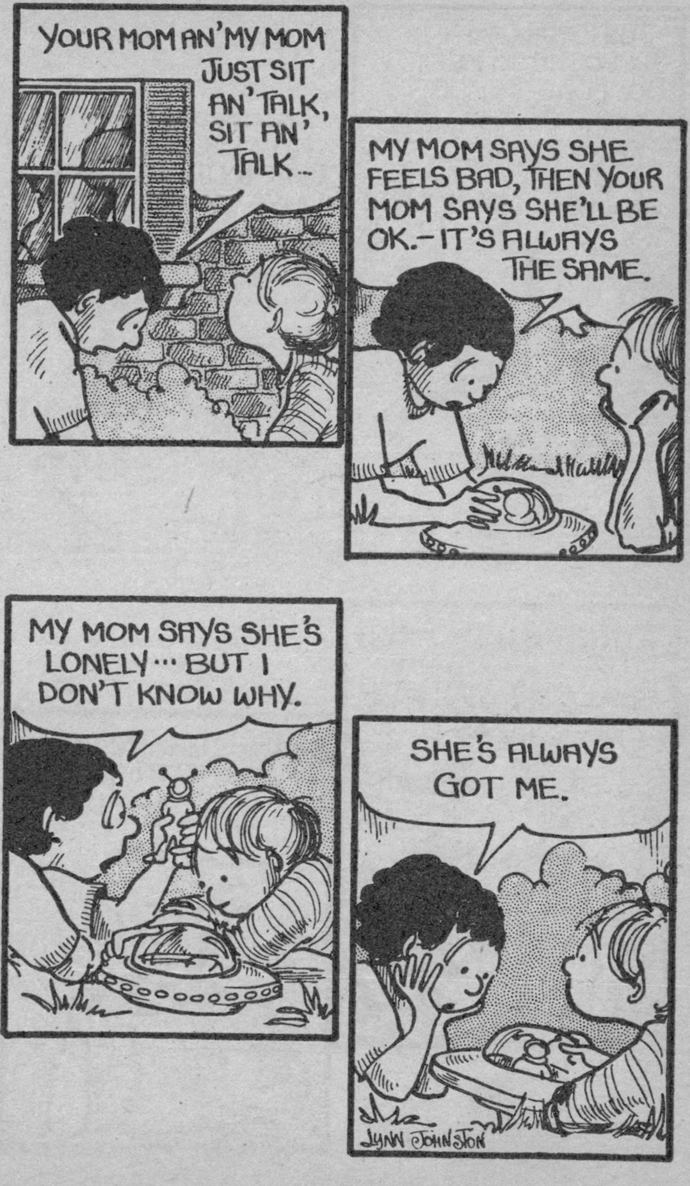
YOUR MOM AN' MY MOM JUST SIT AN' TALK, SIT AN' TALK...
MY MOM SAYS SHE FEELS BAD, THEN YOUR MOM SAYS SHE'LL BE OK.- IT'S ALWAYS THE SAME.
MY MOM SAYS SHE'S LONELY... BUT I DON'T KNOW WHY.
SHE'S ALWAYS GOT ME.
LYNN JOHNSTON

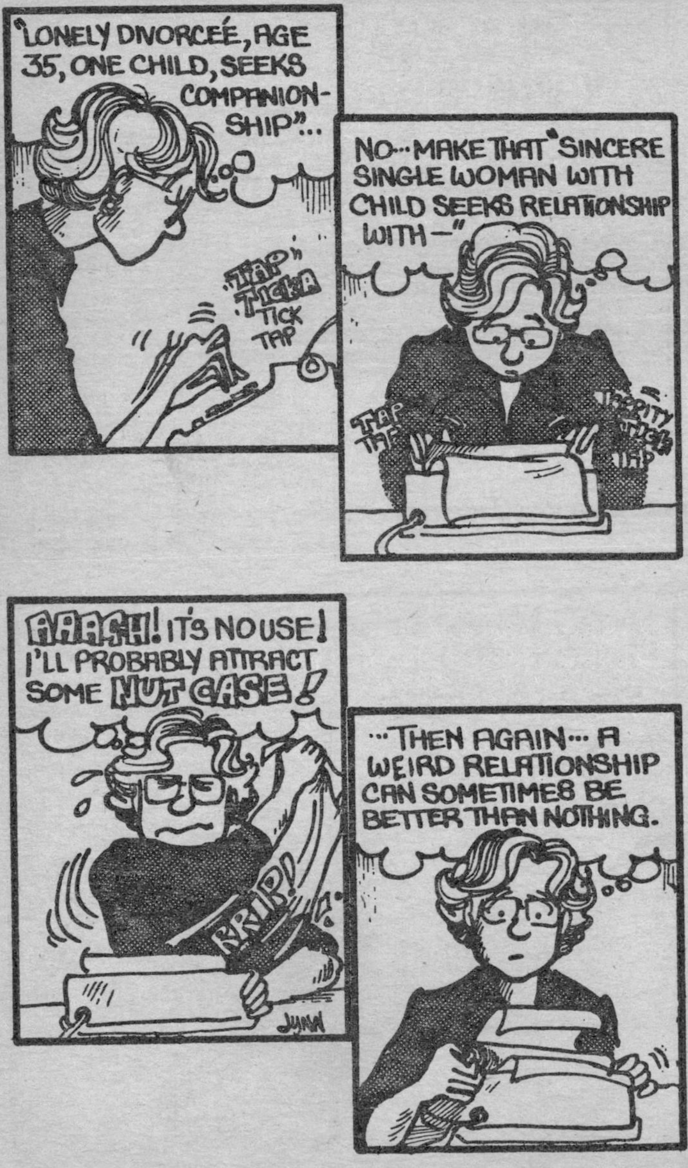

"LONELY DIVORCEÉ, AGE 35, ONE CHILD, SEEKS COMPANIONSHIP"...
TAP TICKA TICK TAP
NO... MAKE THAT "SINCERE SINGLE WOMAN WITH CHILD SEEKS RELATIONSHIP WITH—"
TAP TAP
TAPPITY TICKA TAP
AAAGH! IT'S NO USE! I'LL PROBABLY ATTRACT SOME NUT CASE!
RRIP!
...THEN AGAIN... A WEIRD RELATIONSHIP CAN SOMETIMES BE BETTER THAN NOTHING.

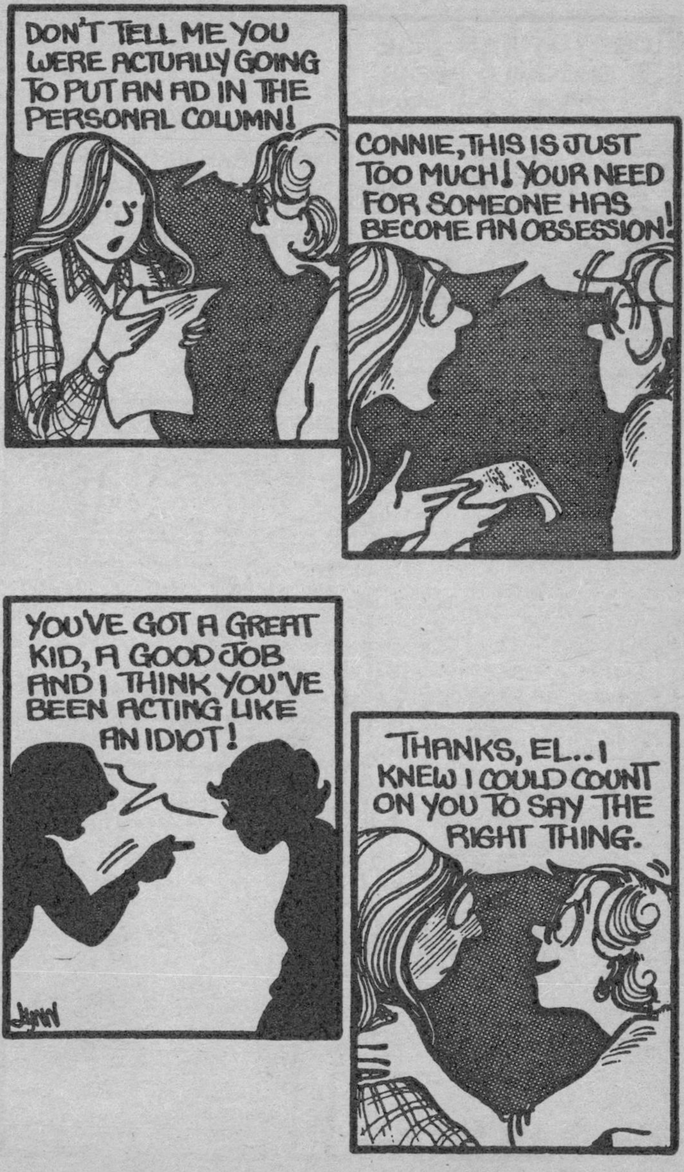
DON'T TELL ME YOU WERE ACTUALLY GOING TO PUT AN AD IN THE PERSONAL COLUMN!
CONNIE, THIS IS JUST TOO MUCH! YOUR NEED FOR SOMEONE HAS BECOME AN OBSESSION!
YOU'VE GOT A GREAT KID, A GOOD JOB AND I THINK YOU'VE BEEN ACTING LIKE AN IDIOT!
THANKS, EL.. I KNEW I COULD COUNT ON YOU TO SAY THE RIGHT THING.

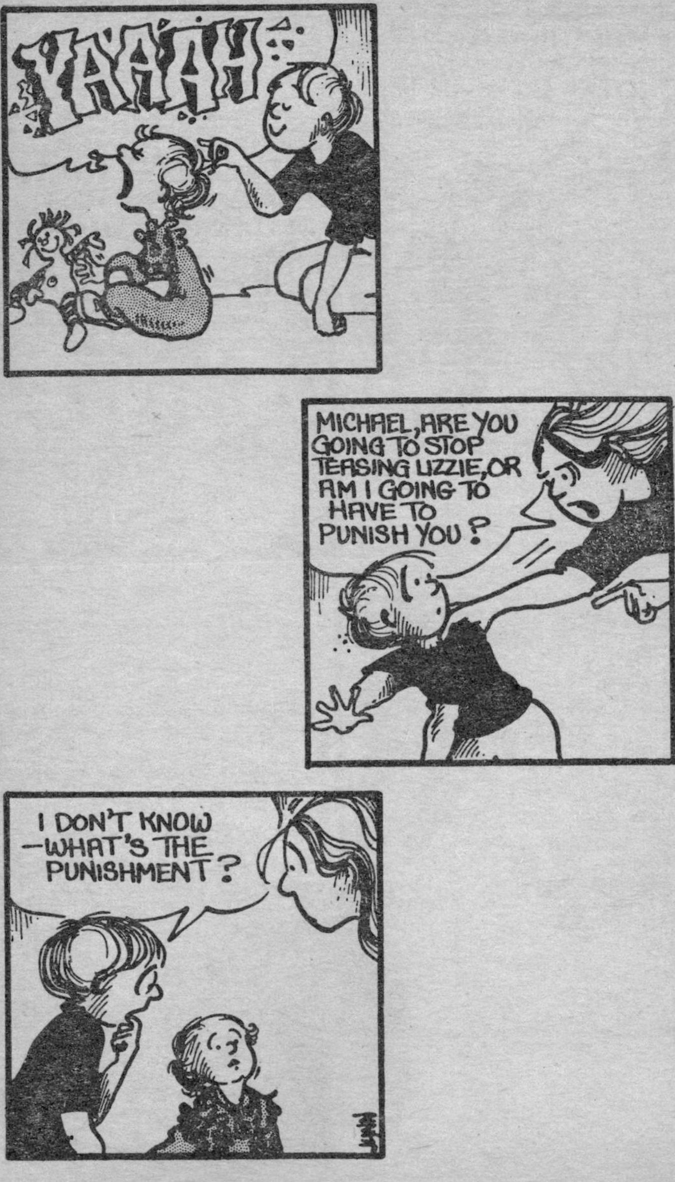
YAAAH
MICHAEL, ARE YOU GOING TO STOP TEASING LIZZIE, OR AM I GOING TO HAVE TO PUNISH YOU?
I DON'T KNOW —WHAT'S THE PUNISHMENT?

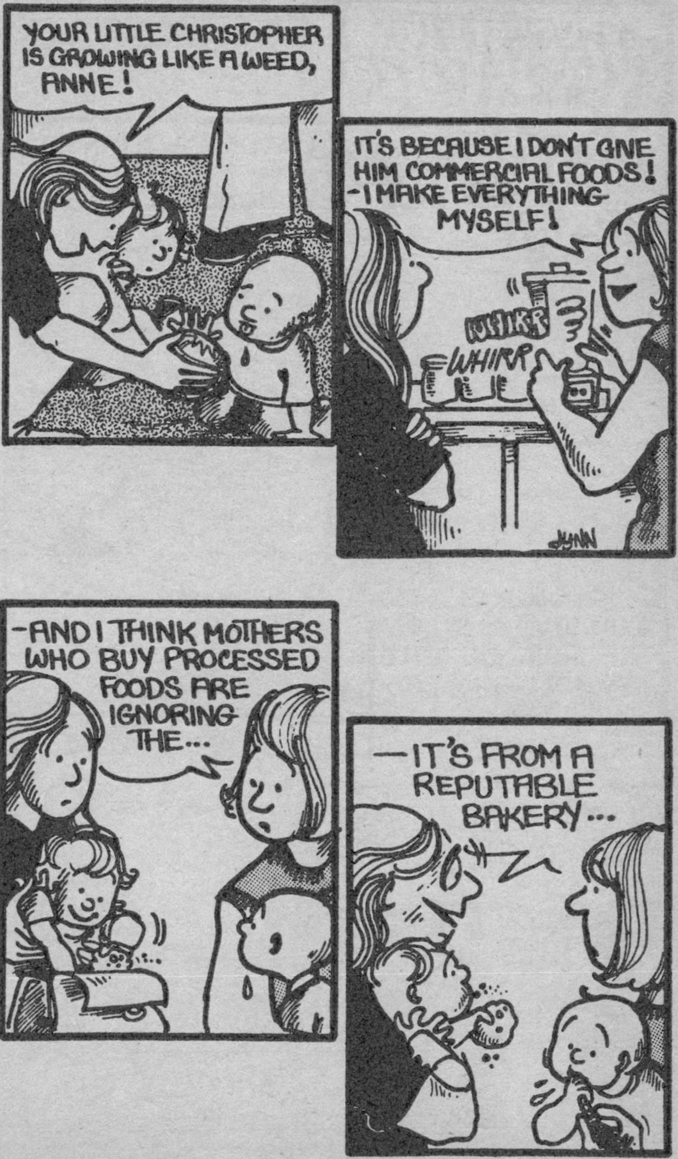
YOUR LITTLE CHRISTOPHER IS GROWING LIKE A WEED, ANNE!
IT'S BECAUSE I DON'T GIVE HIM COMMERCIAL FOODS! - I MAKE EVERYTHING MYSELF!
WHIRR
WHIRR
LYNN
- AND I THINK MOTHERS WHO BUY PROCESSED FOODS ARE IGNORING THE...
— IT'S FROM A REPUTABLE BAKERY...

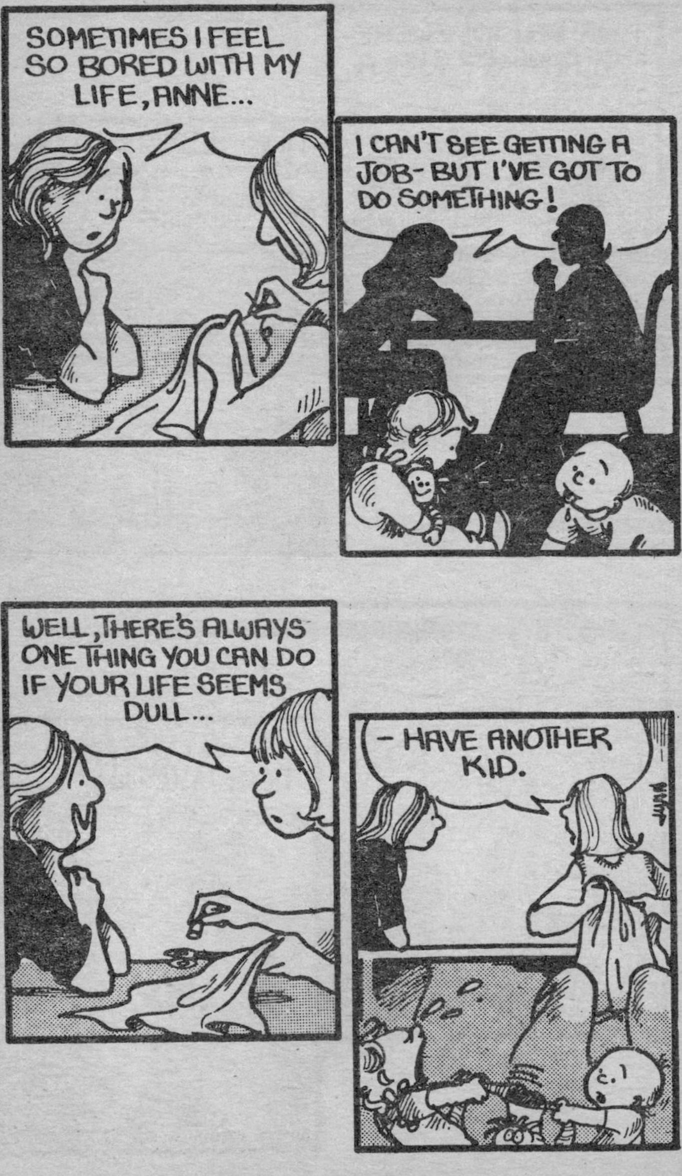
SOMETIMES I FEEL SO BORED WITH MY LIFE, ANNE...
I CAN'T SEE GETTING A JOB- BUT I'VE GOT TO DO SOMETHING!
WELL, THERE'S ALWAYS ONE THING YOU CAN DO IF YOUR LIFE SEEMS DULL...
- HAVE ANOTHER KID.

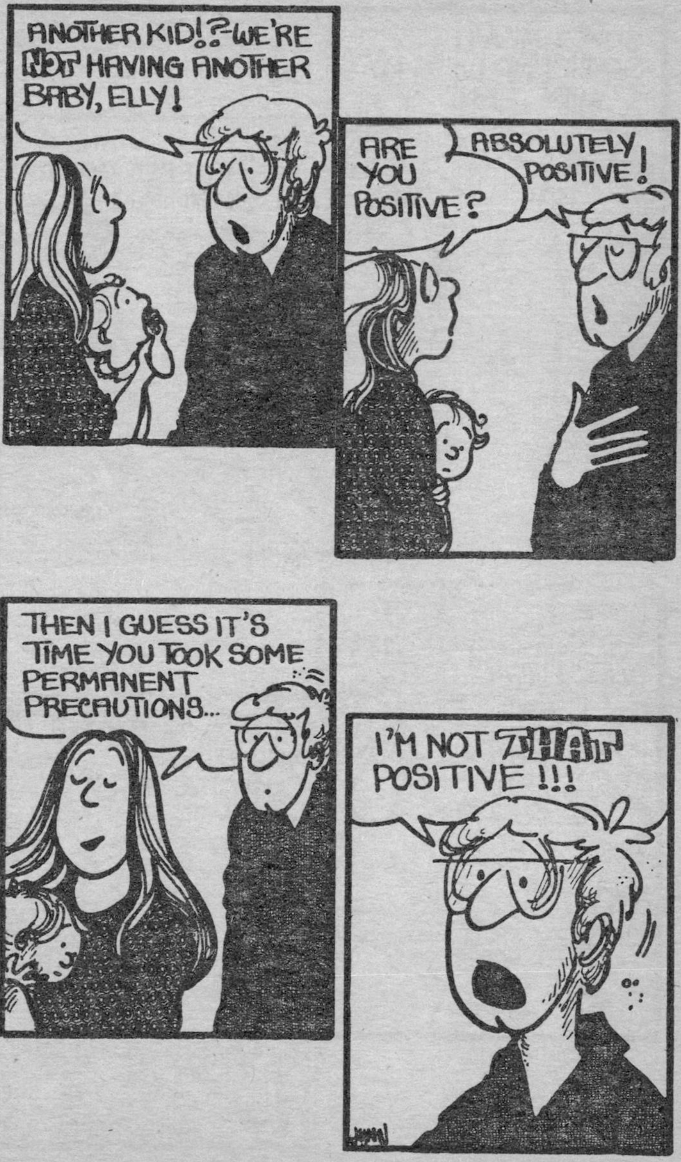
ANOTHER KID!?-WE'RE NOT HAVING ANOTHER BABY, ELLY!
ARE YOU POSITIVE?
ABSOLUTELY POSITIVE!
THEN I GUESS IT'S TIME YOU TOOK SOME PERMANENT PRECAUTIONS...
I'M NOT THAT POSITIVE!!!

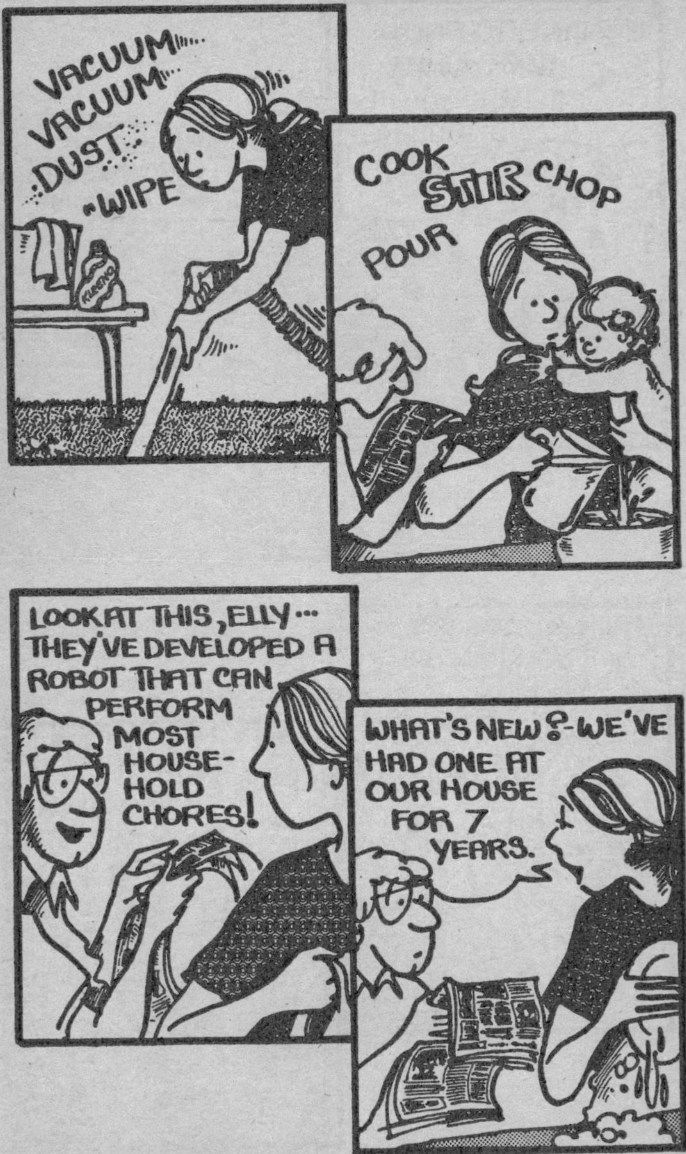
VACUUM
VACUUM
DUST
WIPE
KLEENO
COOK STIR CHOP
POUR
LOOK AT THIS, ELLY... THEY'VE DEVELOPED A ROBOT THAT CAN PERFORM MOST HOUSE-HOLD CHORES!
WHAT'S NEW?-WE'VE HAD ONE AT OUR HOUSE FOR 7 YEARS.

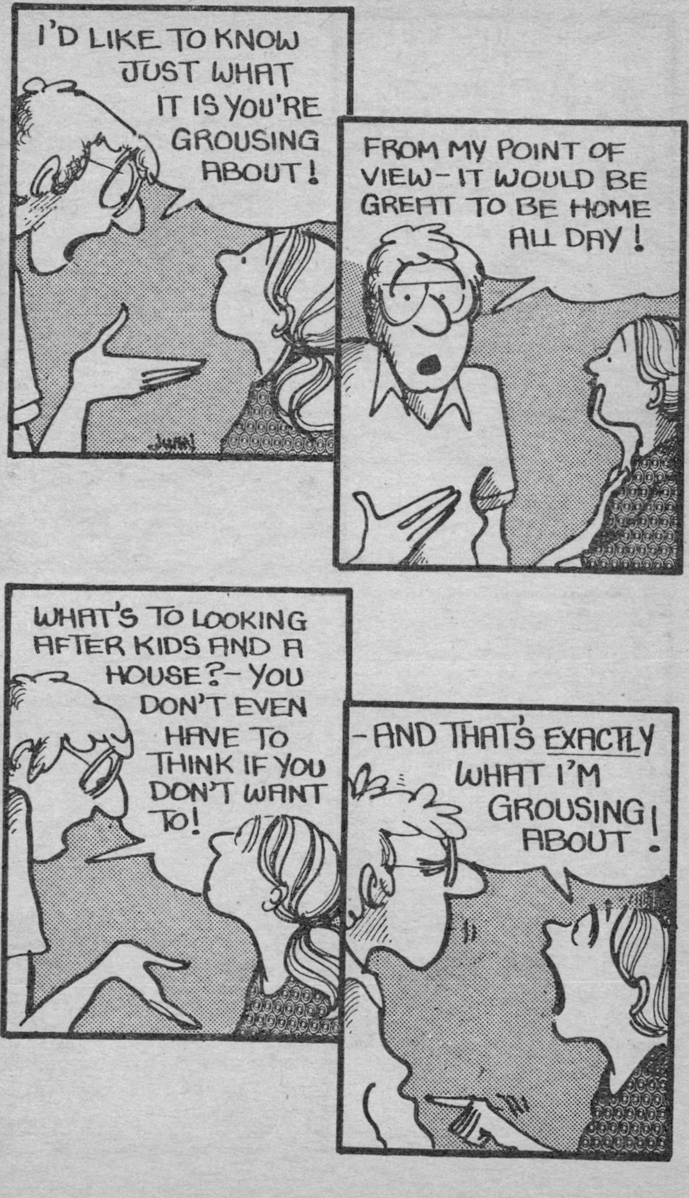
I'D LIKE TO KNOW JUST WHAT IT IS YOU'RE GROUSING ABOUT!
FROM MY POINT OF VIEW- IT WOULD BE GREAT TO BE HOME ALL DAY!
WHAT'S TO LOOKING AFTER KIDS AND A HOUSE?- YOU DON'T EVEN HAVE TO THINK IF YOU DON'T WANT TO!
-AND THAT'S EXACTLY WHAT I'M GROUSING ABOUT!

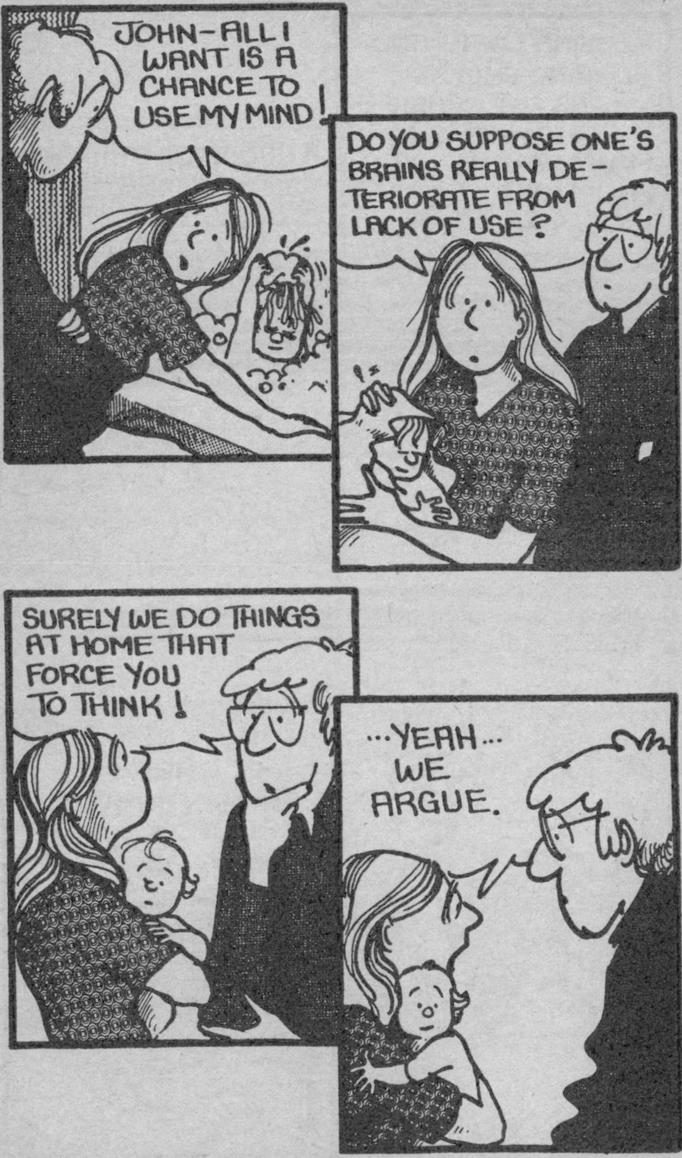
JOHN-ALL I WANT IS A CHANCE TO USE MY MIND!
DO YOU SUPPOSE ONE'S BRAINS REALLY DE-TERIORATE FROM LACK OF USE?
SURELY WE DO THINGS AT HOME THAT FORCE YOU TO THINK!
...YEAH... WE ARGUE.

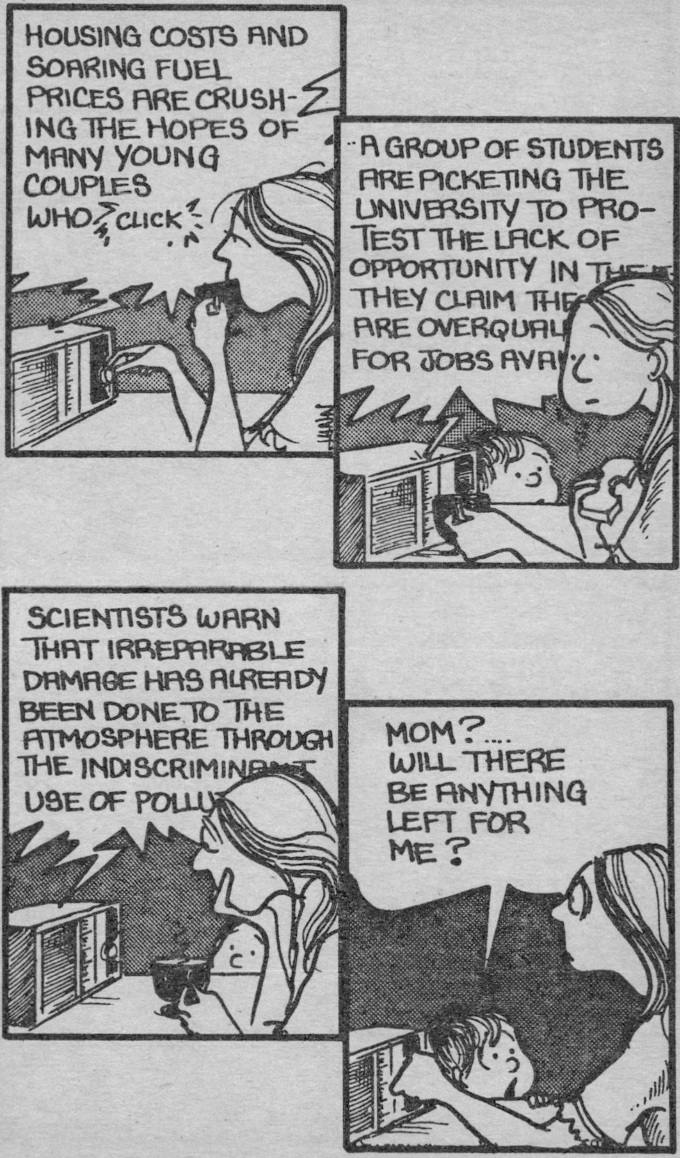
HOUSING COSTS AND SOARING FUEL PRICES ARE CRUSHING THE HOPES OF MANY YOUNG COUPLES WHO
CLICK
..A GROUP OF STUDENTS ARE PICKETING THE UNIVERSITY TO PROTEST THE LACK OF OPPORTUNITY IN TH
THEY CLAIM THE
ARE OVERQUAL
FOR JOBS AVA
SCIENTISTS WARN THAT IRREPARABLE DAMAGE HAS ALREADY BEEN DONE TO THE ATMOSPHERE THROUGH THE INDISCRIMIN
USE OF POLLU
MOM?.... WILL THERE BE ANYTHING LEFT FOR ME?

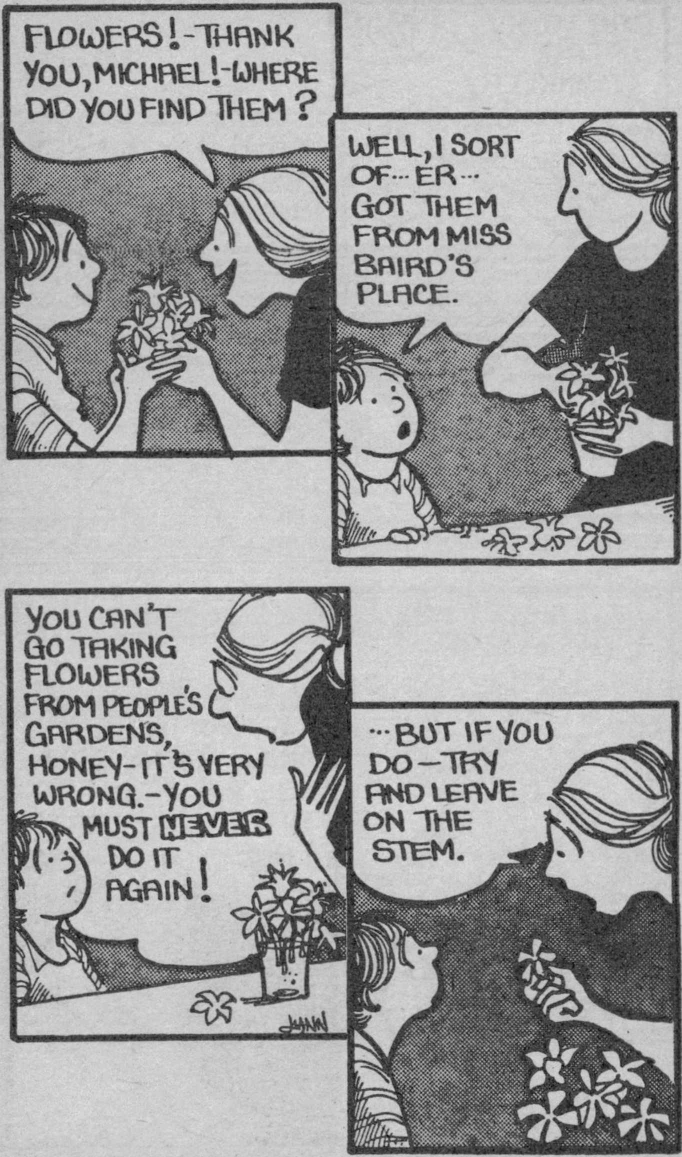
FLOWERS!-THANK YOU, MICHAEL!-WHERE DID YOU FIND THEM?
WELL, I SORT OF... ER... GOT THEM FROM MISS BAIRD'S PLACE.
YOU CAN'T GO TAKING FLOWERS FROM PEOPLE'S GARDENS, HONEY-IT'S VERY WRONG.-YOU MUST NEVER DO IT AGAIN!
LYNN
...BUT IF YOU DO-TRY AND LEAVE ON THE STEM.

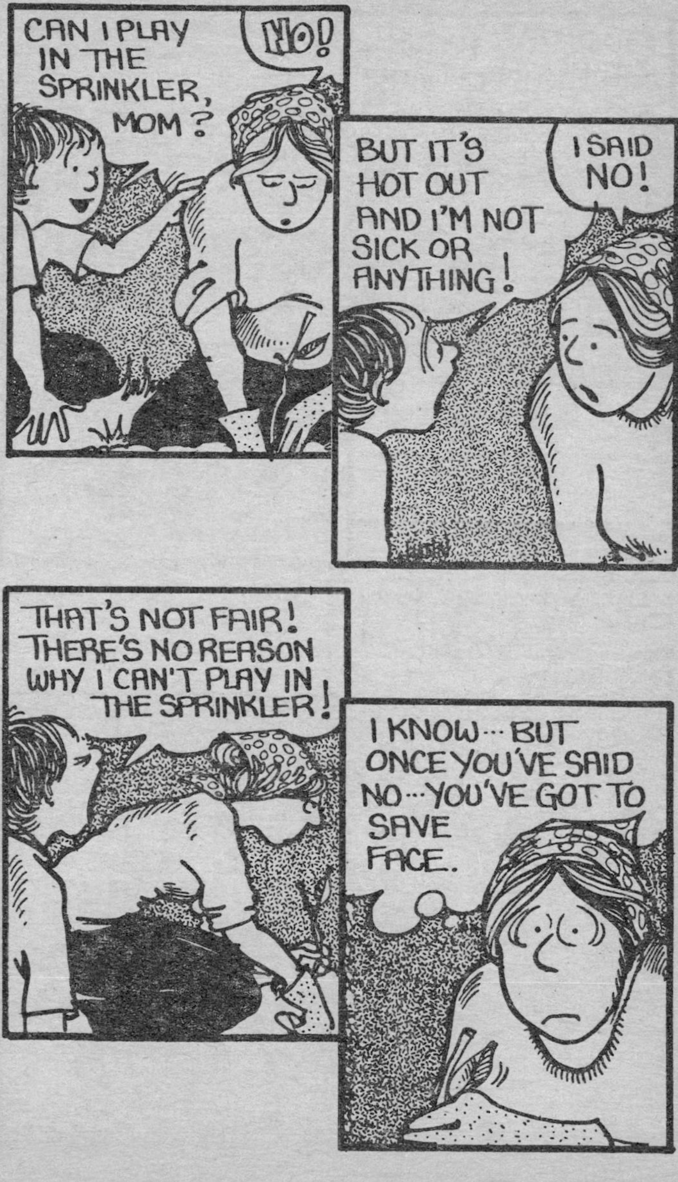
CAN I PLAY IN THE SPRINKLER, MOM?
NO!
BUT IT'S HOT OUT AND I'M NOT SICK OR ANYTHING!
I SAID NO!
THAT'S NOT FAIR! THERE'S NO REASON WHY I CAN'T PLAY IN THE SPRINKLER!
I KNOW... BUT ONCE YOU'VE SAID NO... YOU'VE GOT TO SAVE FACE.

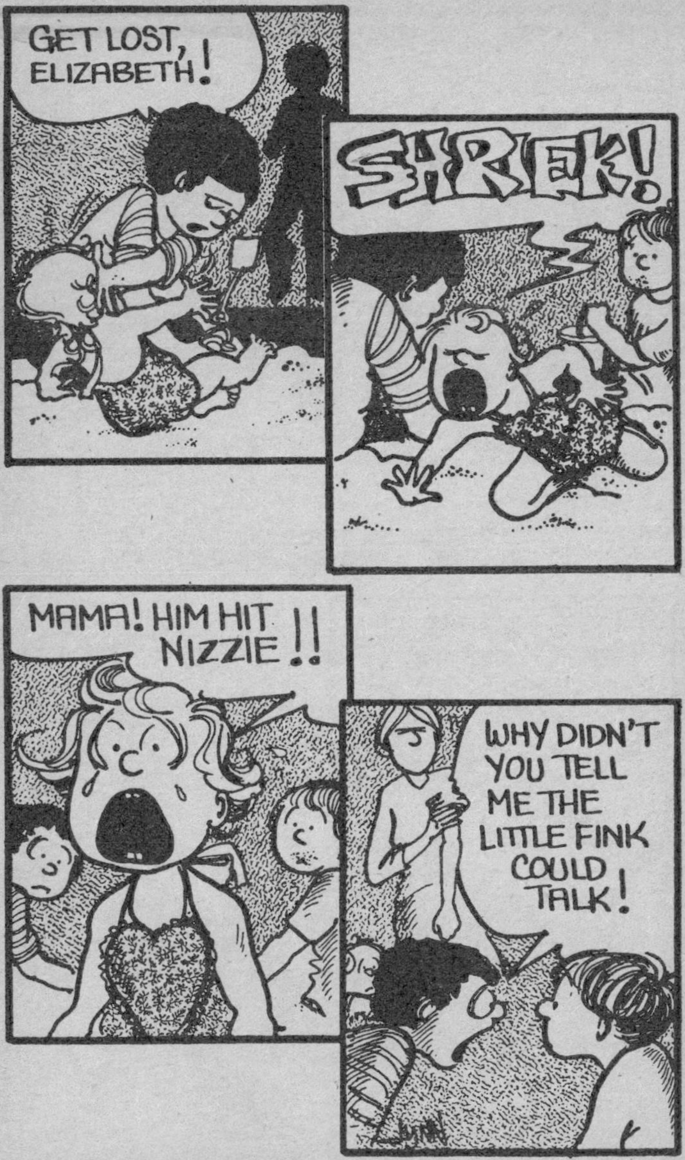
GET LOST, ELIZABETH!
SHREK!
MAMA! HIM HIT NIZZIE!!
WHY DIDN'T YOU TELL ME THE LITTLE FINK COULD TALK!

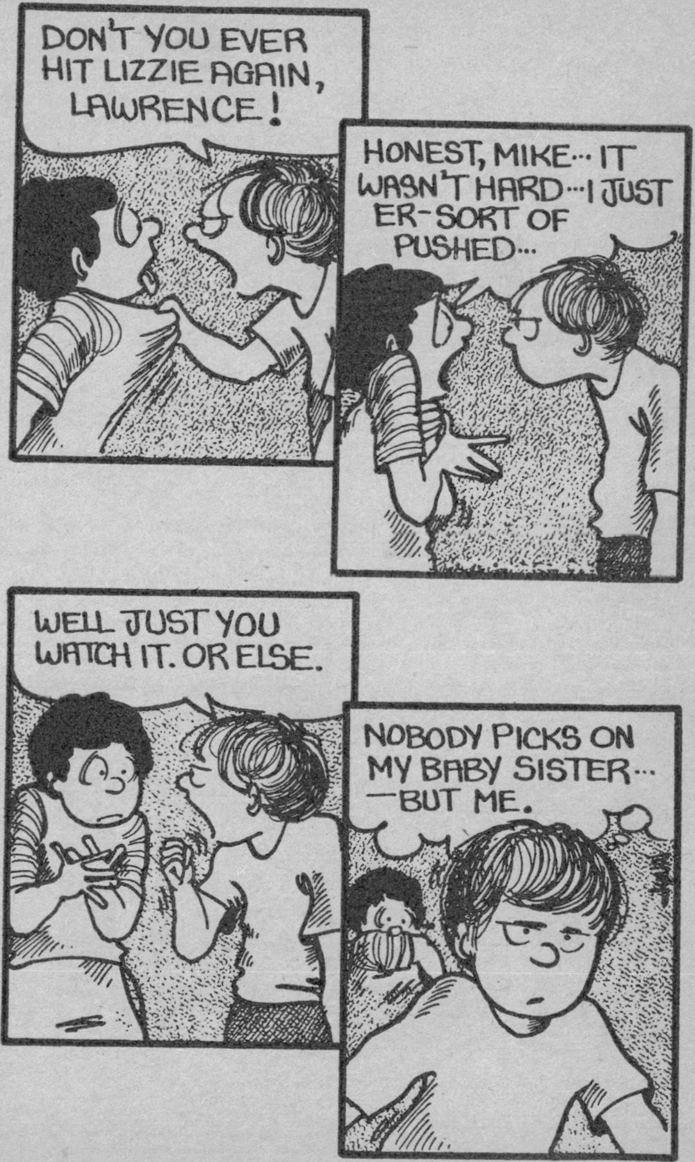
DON'T YOU EVER HIT LIZZIE AGAIN, LAWRENCE!
HONEST, MIKE... IT WASN'T HARD... I JUST ER-SORT OF PUSHED...
WELL JUST YOU WATCH IT. OR ELSE.
NOBODY PICKS ON MY BABY SISTER... —BUT ME.

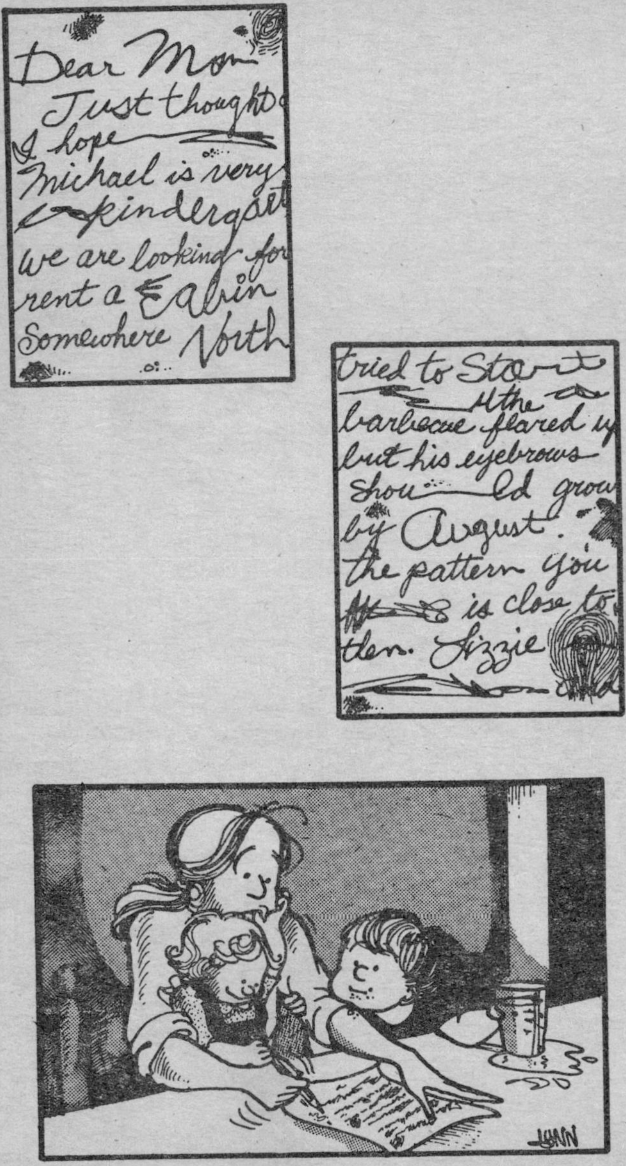
Dear Mom
Just thought
I hope
Michael is very
kindergart
we are looking for
rent a cabin
Somewhere North
tried to Start
the
barbecue flared u
but his eyebrows
should grow
by August.
the pattern you
is close to
then. Lizzie
LYNN

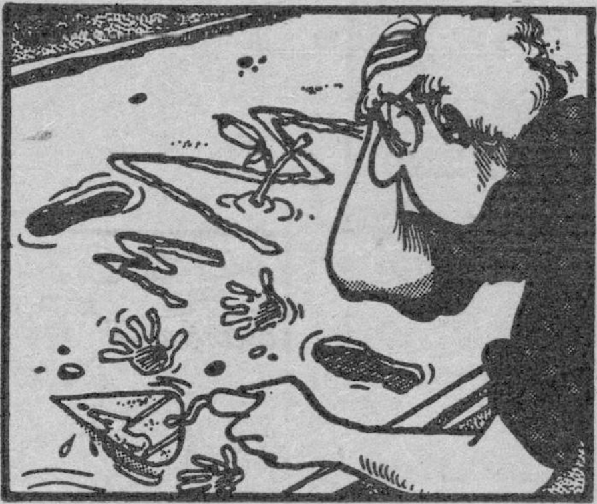

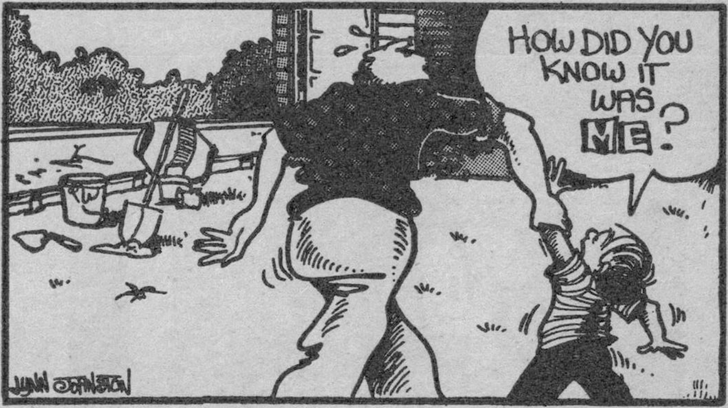
HOW DID YOU KNOW IT WAS ME?
LYNN JOHNSTON

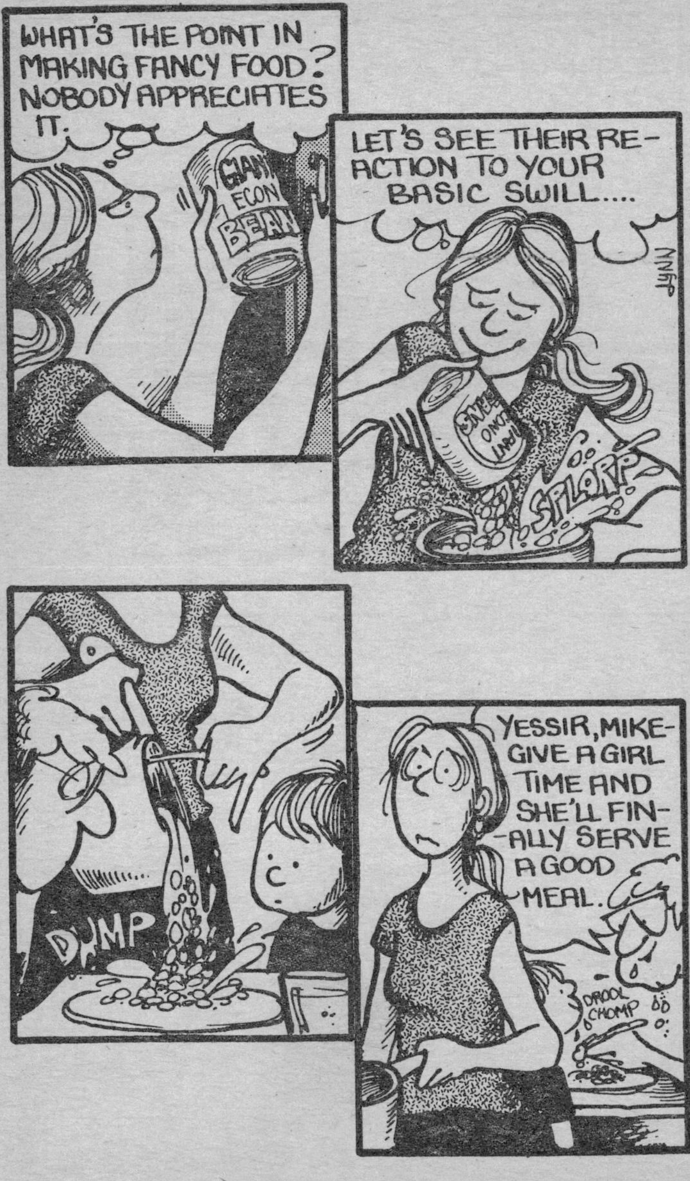
WHAT'S THE POINT IN MAKING FANCY FOOD? NOBODY APPRECIATES IT.
GIANT ECON BEAN
LET'S SEE THEIR RE-ACTION TO YOUR BASIC SWILL....
Lynn
SPLORP!
DUMP
YESSIR, MIKE- GIVE A GIRL TIME AND SHE'LL FIN-ALLY SERVE A GOOD MEAL.
DROOL CHOMP

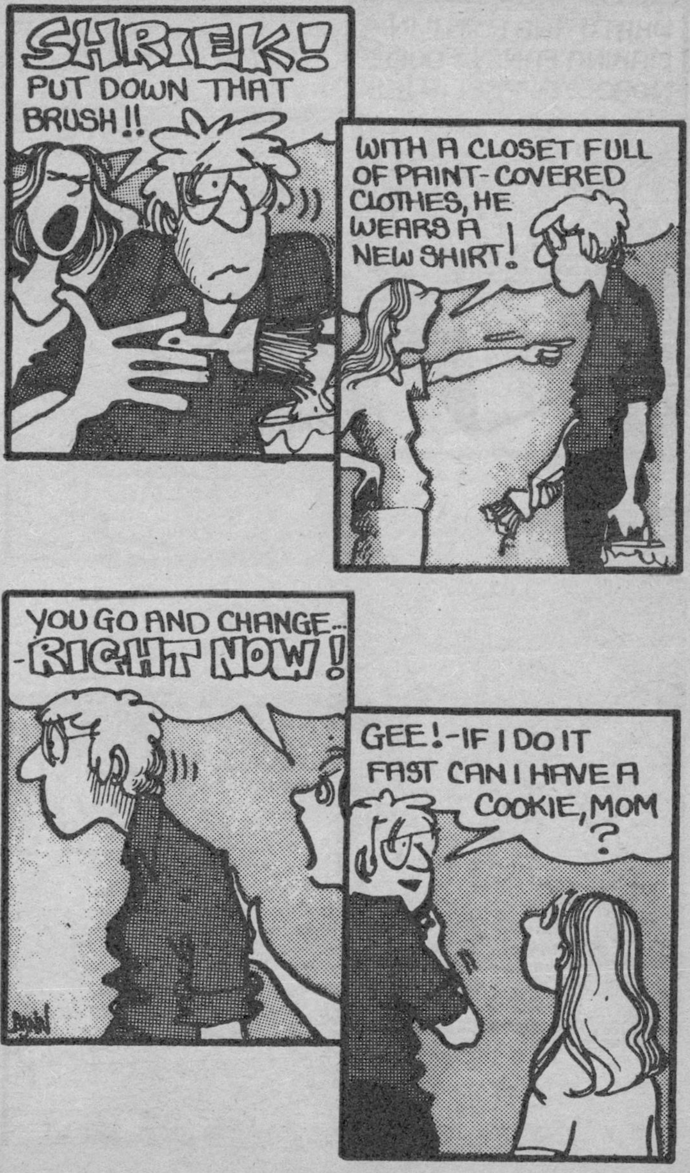
SHRIEK!
PUT DOWN THAT BRUSH!!
WITH A CLOSET FULL OF PAINT-COVERED CLOTHES, HE WEARS A NEW SHIRT!
YOU GO AND CHANGE... -RIGHT NOW!
GEE!-IF I DO IT FAST CAN I HAVE A COOKIE, MOM?

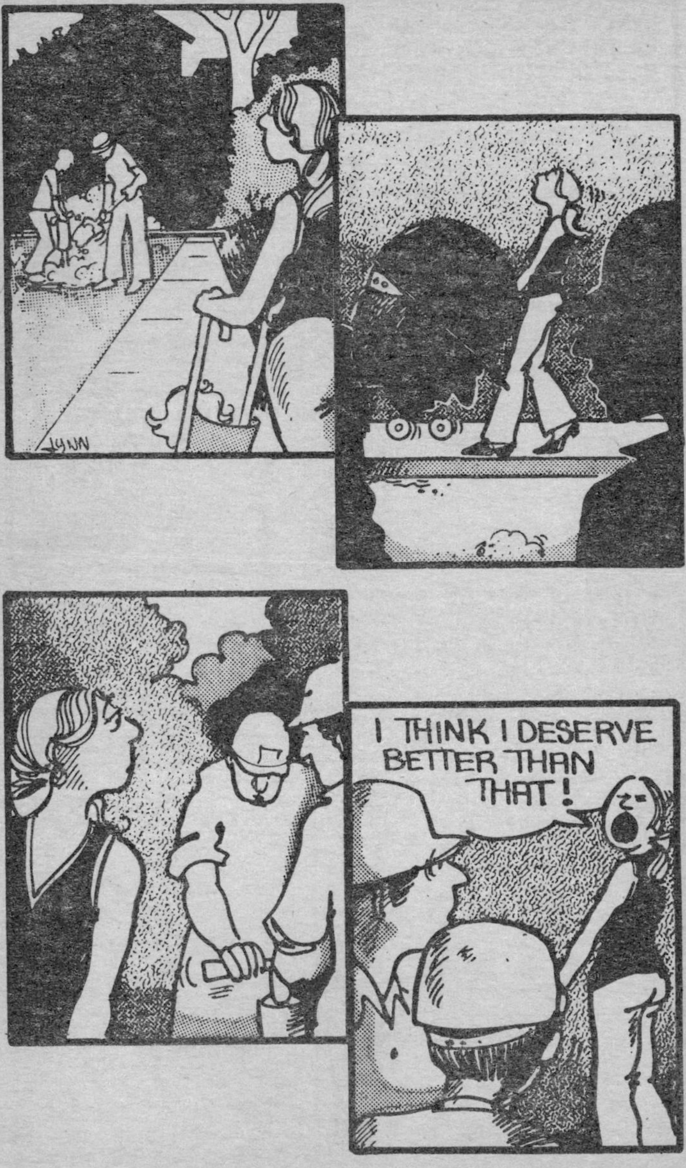
I THINK I DESERVE BETTER THAN THAT!

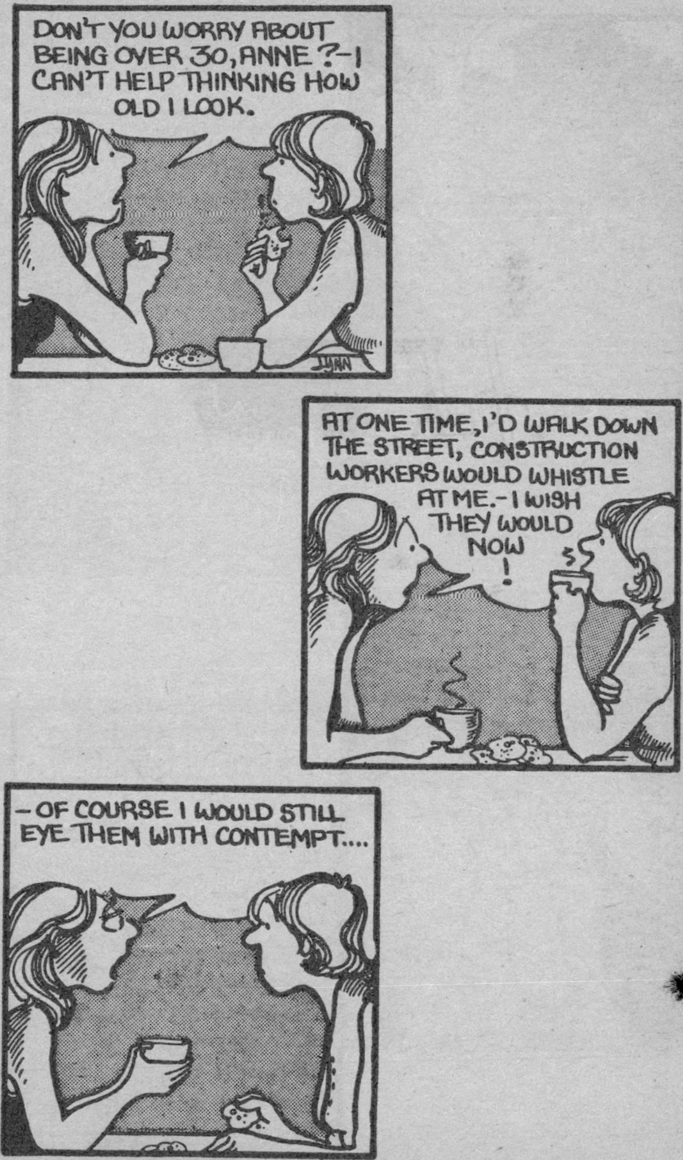
DON'T YOU WORRY ABOUT BEING OVER 30, ANNE?—I CAN'T HELP THINKING HOW OLD I LOOK.
AT ONE TIME, I'D WALK DOWN THE STREET, CONSTRUCTION WORKERS WOULD WHISTLE AT ME.—I WISH THEY WOULD NOW!
—OF COURSE I WOULD STILL EYE THEM WITH CONTEMPT....

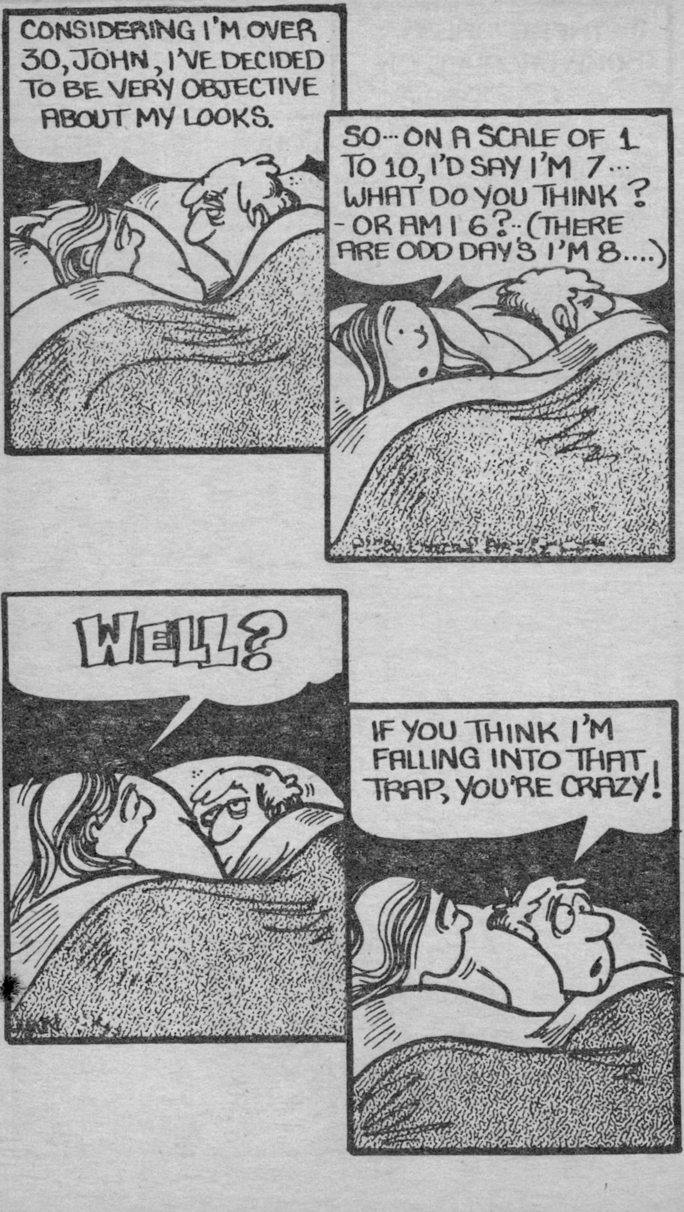
CONSIDERING I'M OVER 30, JOHN, I'VE DECIDED TO BE VERY OBJECTIVE ABOUT MY LOOKS.
SO··· ON A SCALE OF 1 TO 10, I'D SAY I'M 7··· WHAT DO YOU THINK? - OR AM I 6?·· (THERE ARE ODD DAY'S I'M 8....)
WELL?
IF YOU THINK I'M FALLING INTO THAT TRAP, YOU'RE CRAZY!

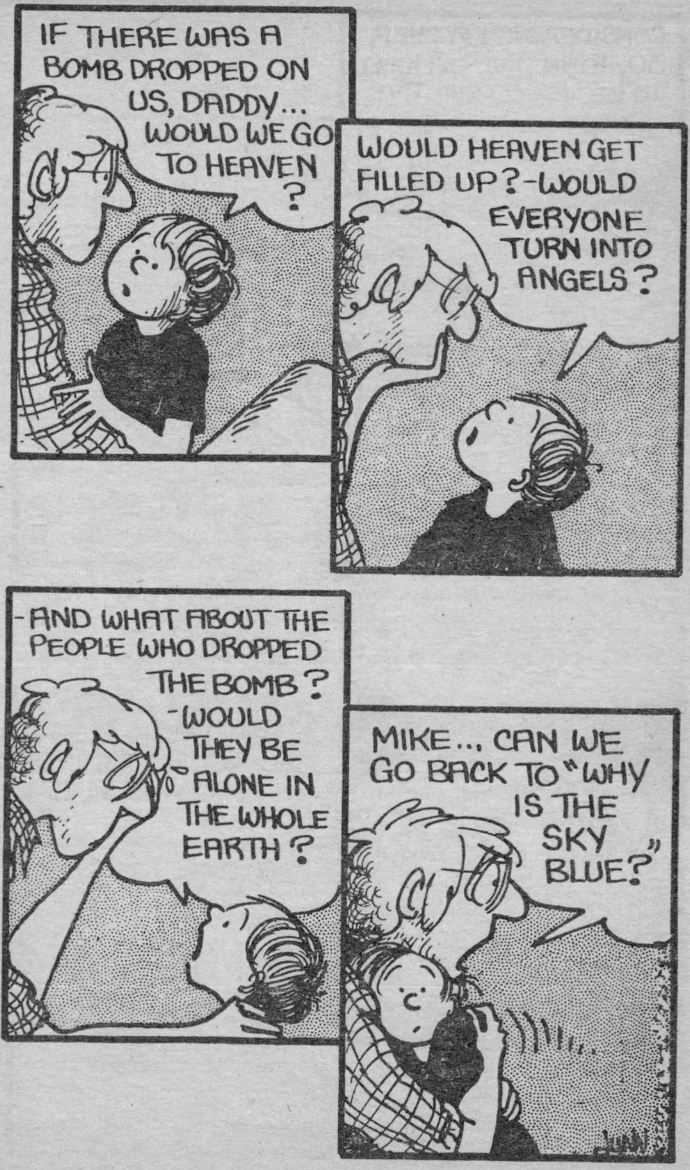
IF THERE WAS A BOMB DROPPED ON US, DADDY... WOULD WE GO TO HEAVEN?
WOULD HEAVEN GET FILLED UP?-WOULD EVERYONE TURN INTO ANGELS?
-AND WHAT ABOUT THE PEOPLE WHO DROPPED THE BOMB? -WOULD THEY BE ALONE IN THE WHOLE EARTH?
MIKE..., CAN WE GO BACK TO "WHY IS THE SKY BLUE?"

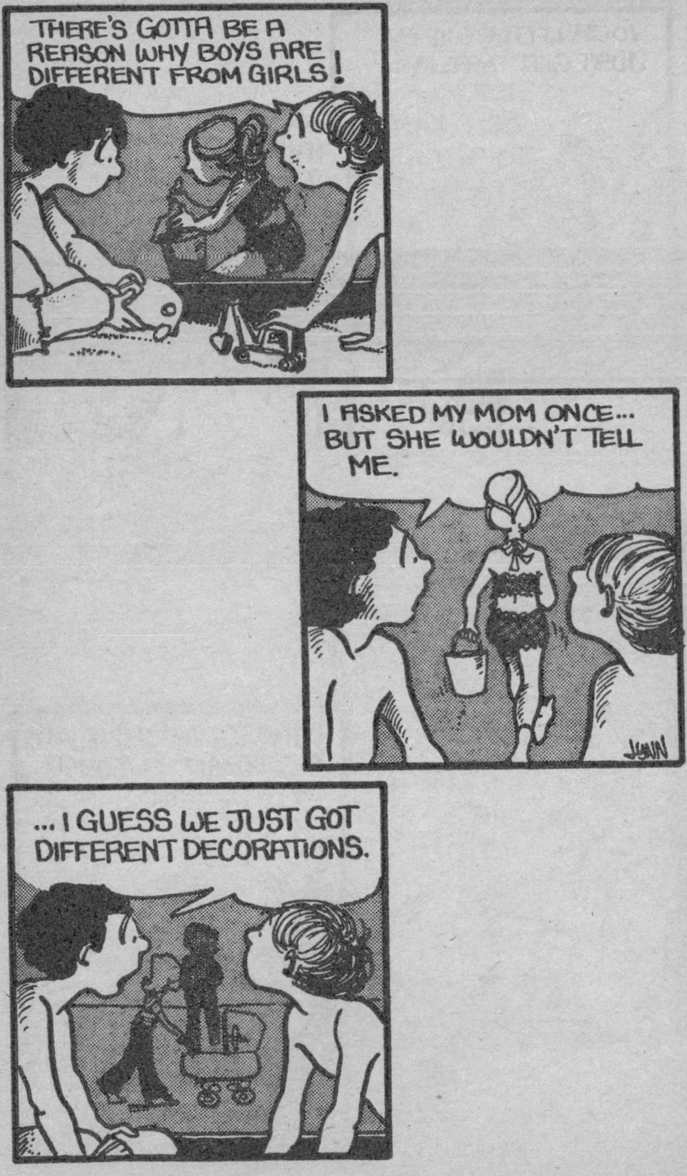
THERE'S GOTTA BE A REASON WHY BOYS ARE DIFFERENT FROM GIRLS!
I ASKED MY MOM ONCE... BUT SHE WOULDN'T TELL ME.
...I GUESS WE JUST GOT DIFFERENT DECORATIONS.

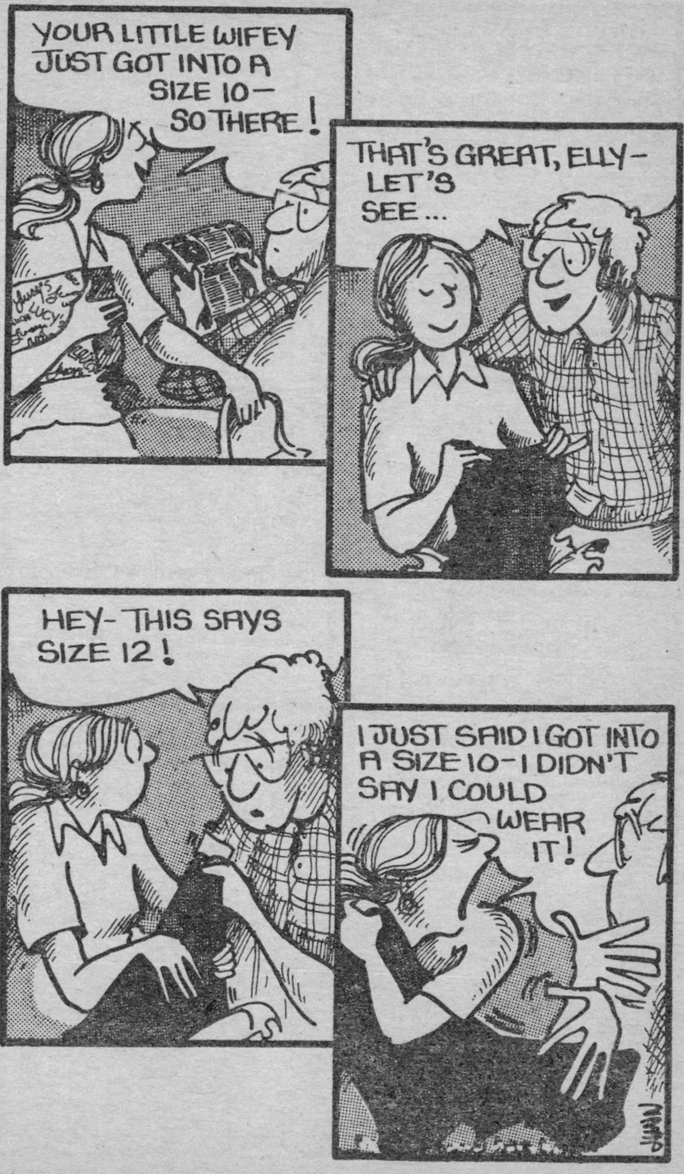
YOUR LITTLE WIFEY JUST GOT INTO A SIZE 10— SO THERE!
THAT'S GREAT, ELLY— LET'S SEE...
HEY- THIS SAYS SIZE 12!
I JUST SAID I GOT INTO A SIZE 10—I DIDN'T SAY I COULD WEAR IT!

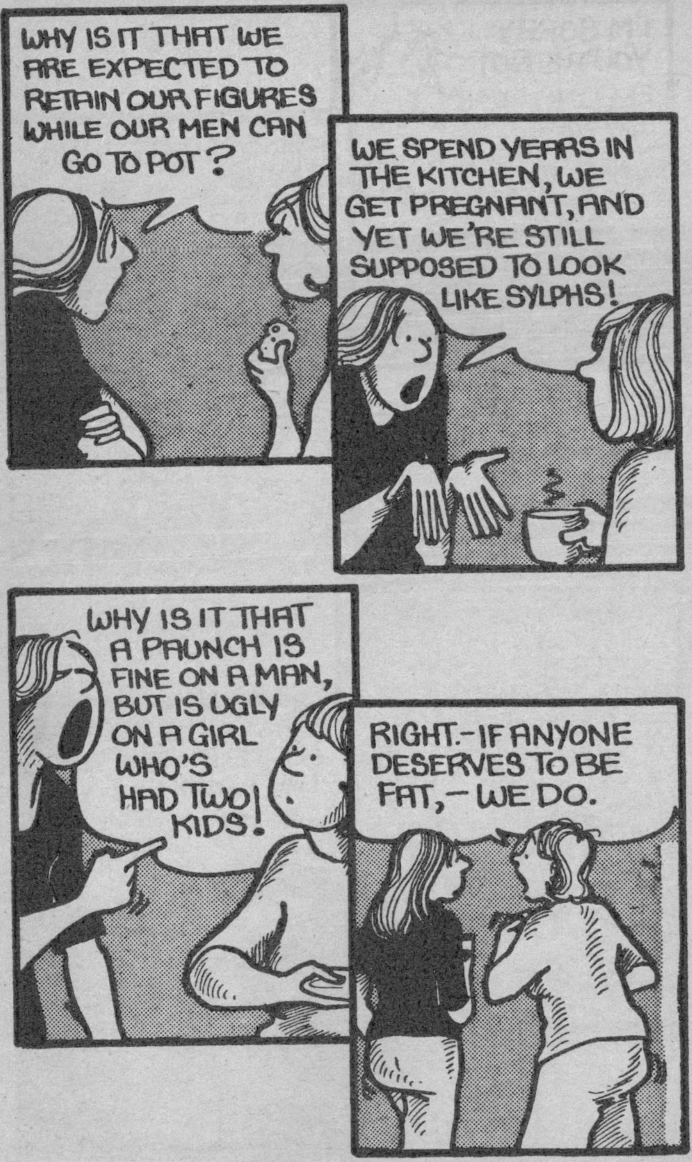
WHY IS IT THAT WE ARE EXPECTED TO RETAIN OUR FIGURES WHILE OUR MEN CAN GO TO POT?
WE SPEND YEARS IN THE KITCHEN, WE GET PREGNANT, AND YET WE'RE STILL SUPPOSED TO LOOK LIKE SYLPHS!
WHY IS IT THAT A PAUNCH IS FINE ON A MAN, BUT IS UGLY ON A GIRL WHO'S HAD TWO KIDS!
RIGHT.-IF ANYONE DESERVES TO BE FAT,-WE DO.

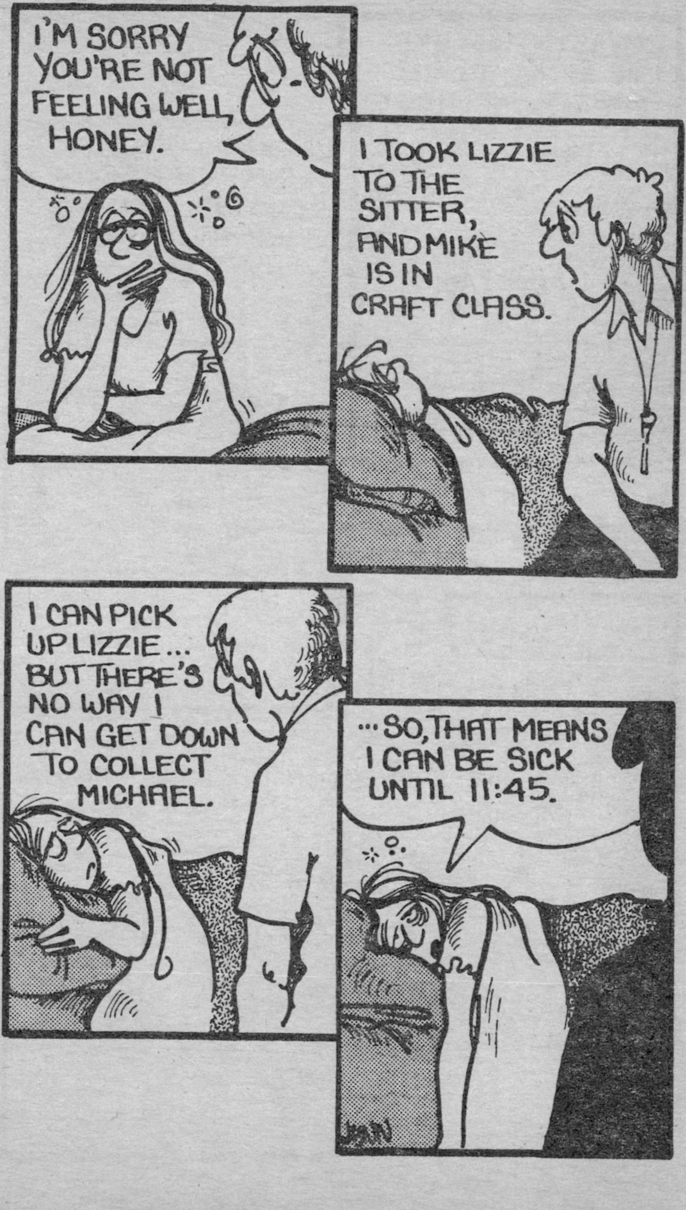
I'M SORRY YOU'RE NOT FEELING WELL, HONEY.
I TOOK LIZZIE TO THE SITTER, AND MIKE IS IN CRAFT CLASS.
I CAN PICK UP LIZZIE... BUT THERE'S NO WAY I CAN GET DOWN TO COLLECT MICHAEL.
...SO, THAT MEANS I CAN BE SICK UNTIL 11:45.

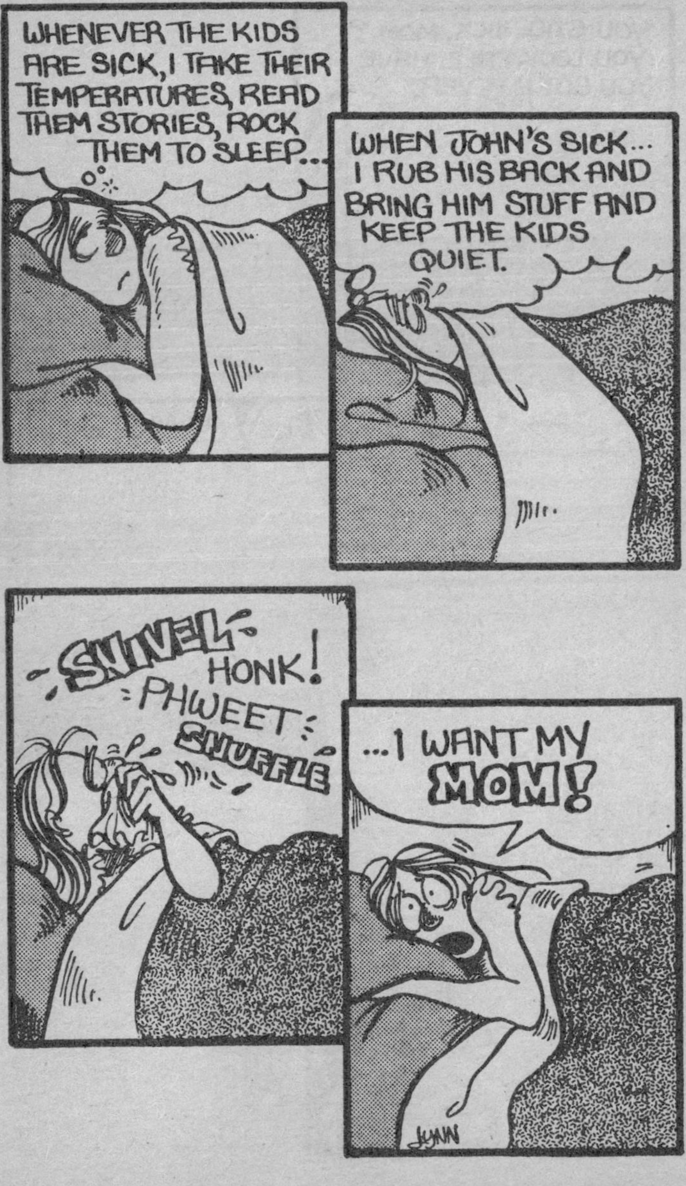
WHENEVER THE KIDS ARE SICK, I TAKE THEIR TEMPERATURES, READ THEM STORIES, ROCK THEM TO SLEEP...
WHEN JOHN'S SICK... I RUB HIS BACK AND BRING HIM STUFF AND KEEP THE KIDS QUIET.
SNIVEL
HONK!
PHWEET
SNUFFLE
...I WANT MY MOM!
LYNN

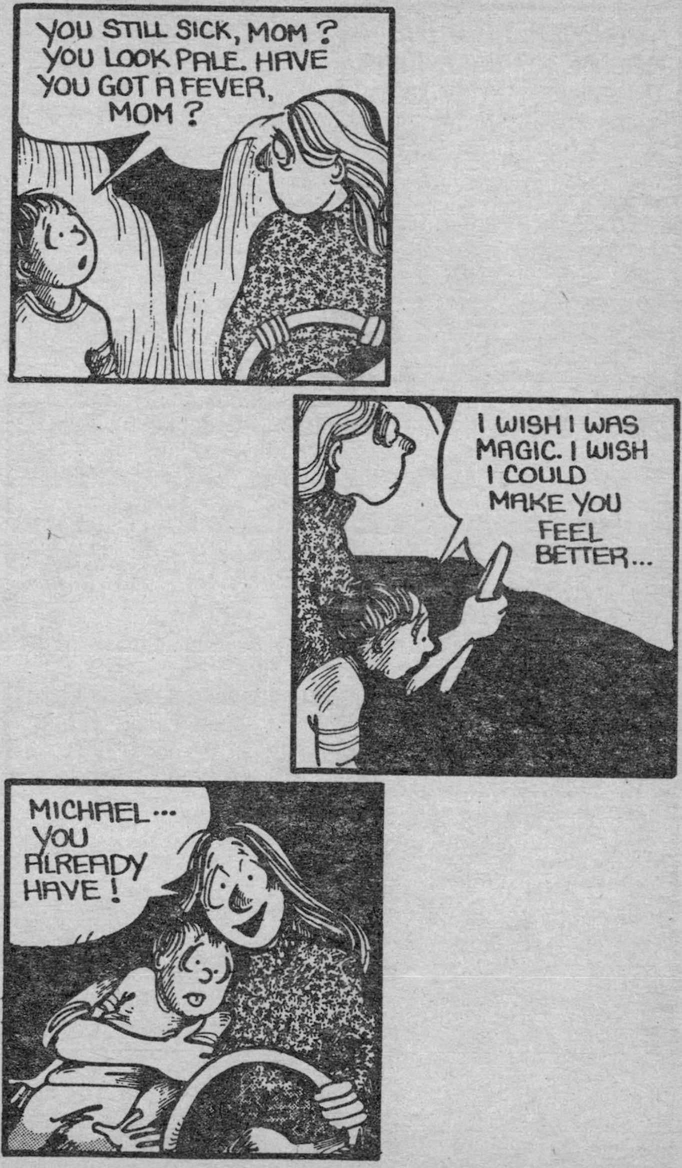
YOU STILL SICK, MOM ? YOU LOOK PALE. HAVE YOU GOT A FEVER, MOM ?
I WISH I WAS MAGIC. I WISH I COULD MAKE YOU FEEL BETTER...
MICHAEL... YOU ALREADY HAVE !

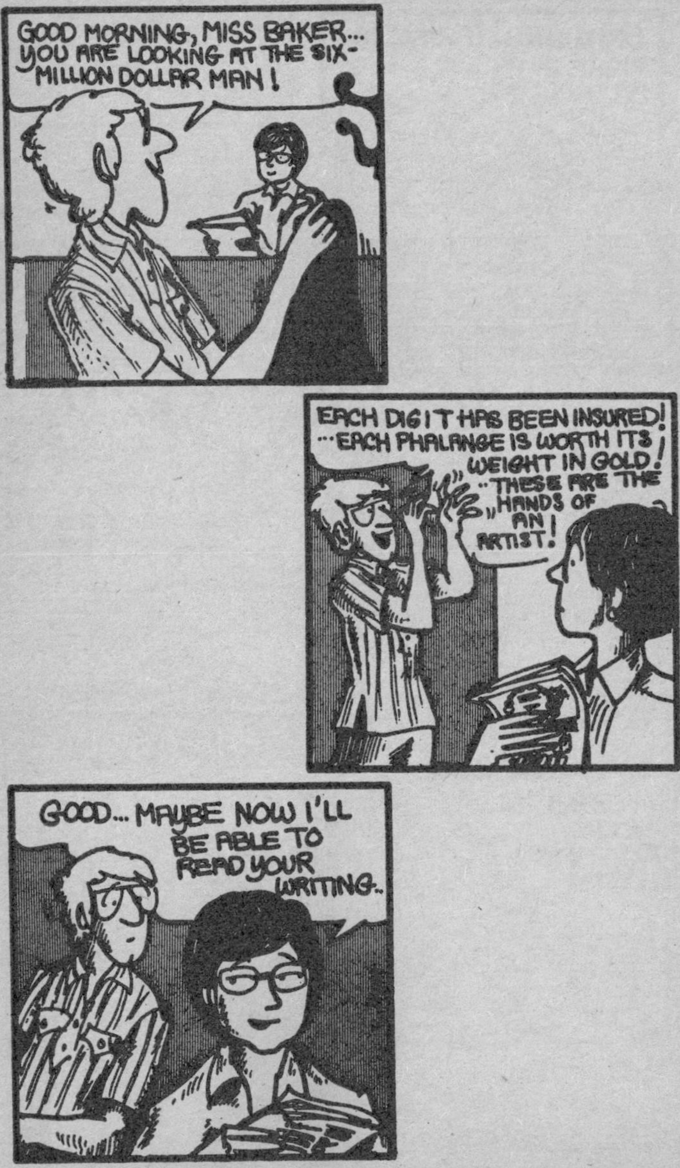
GOOD MORNING, MISS BAKER... YOU ARE LOOKING AT THE SIX-MILLION DOLLAR MAN!
EACH DIGIT HAS BEEN INSURED! ...EACH PHALANGE IS WORTH ITS WEIGHT IN GOLD! ...THESE ARE THE HANDS OF AN ARTIST!
GOOD... MAYBE NOW I'LL BE ABLE TO READ YOUR WRITING..

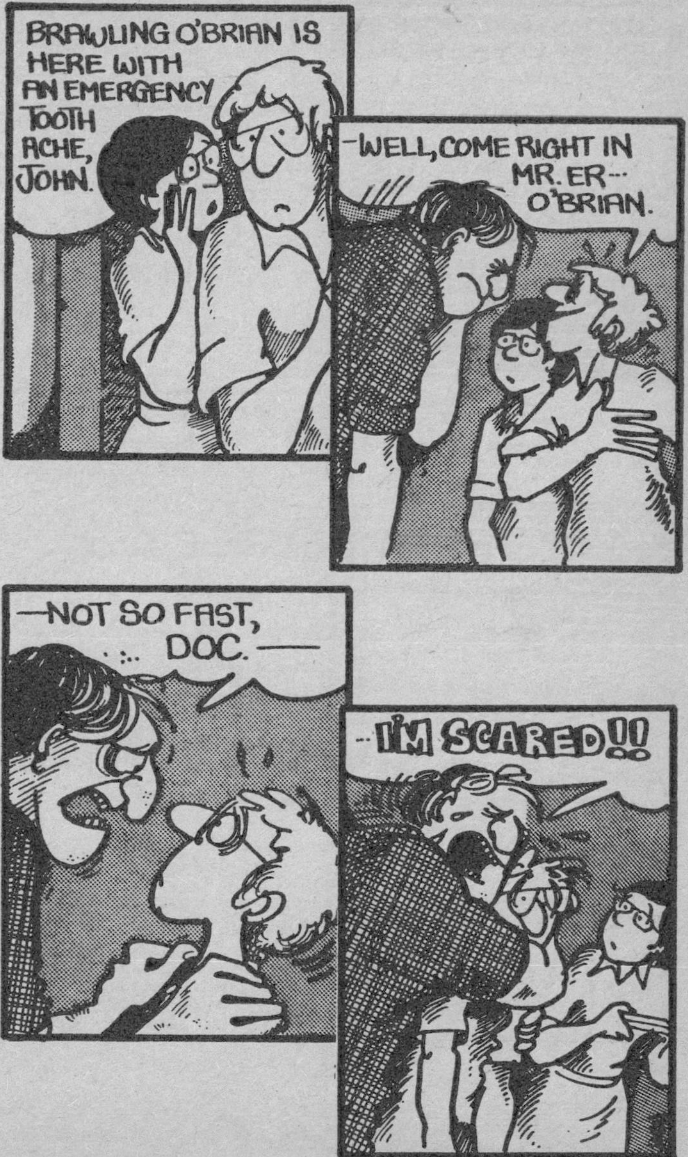
BRAWLING O'BRIAN IS HERE WITH AN EMERGENCY TOOTH ACHE, JOHN.
—WELL, COME RIGHT IN MR. ER— O'BRIAN.
—NOT SO FAST, DOC.—
—I'M SCARED!!

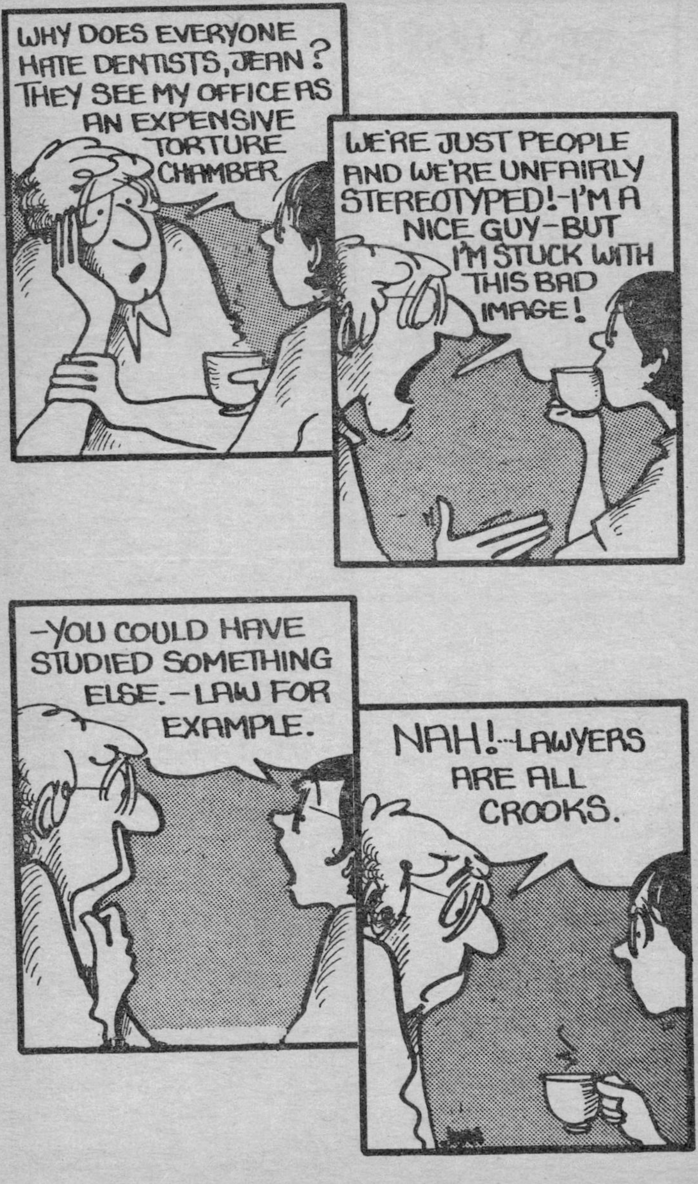
WHY DOES EVERYONE HATE DENTISTS, JEAN? THEY SEE MY OFFICE AS AN EXPENSIVE TORTURE CHAMBER.
WE'RE JUST PEOPLE AND WE'RE UNFAIRLY STEREOTYPED!–I'M A NICE GUY–BUT I'M STUCK WITH THIS BAD IMAGE!
–YOU COULD HAVE STUDIED SOMETHING ELSE.–LAW FOR EXAMPLE.
NAH!...LAWYERS ARE ALL CROOKS.

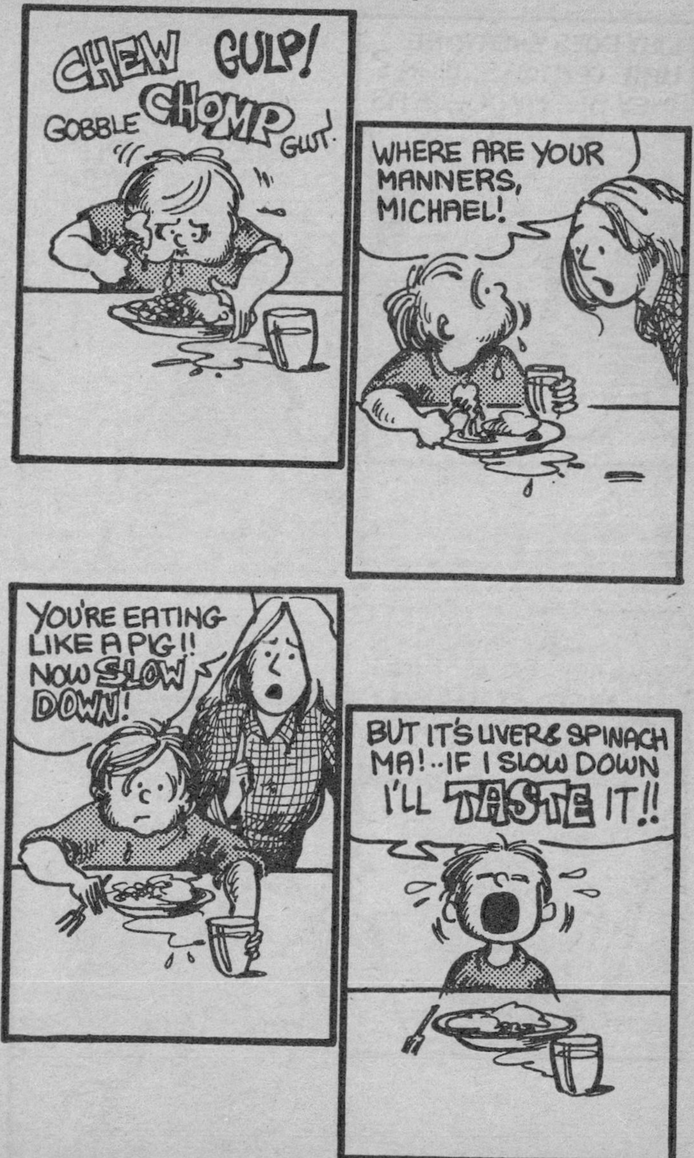
CHEW GULP!
GOBBLE CHOMP GLUT.
WHERE ARE YOUR MANNERS, MICHAEL!
YOU'RE EATING LIKE A PIG!! NOW SLOW DOWN!
BUT IT'S LIVER & SPINACH MA!..IF I SLOW DOWN I'LL TASTE IT!!

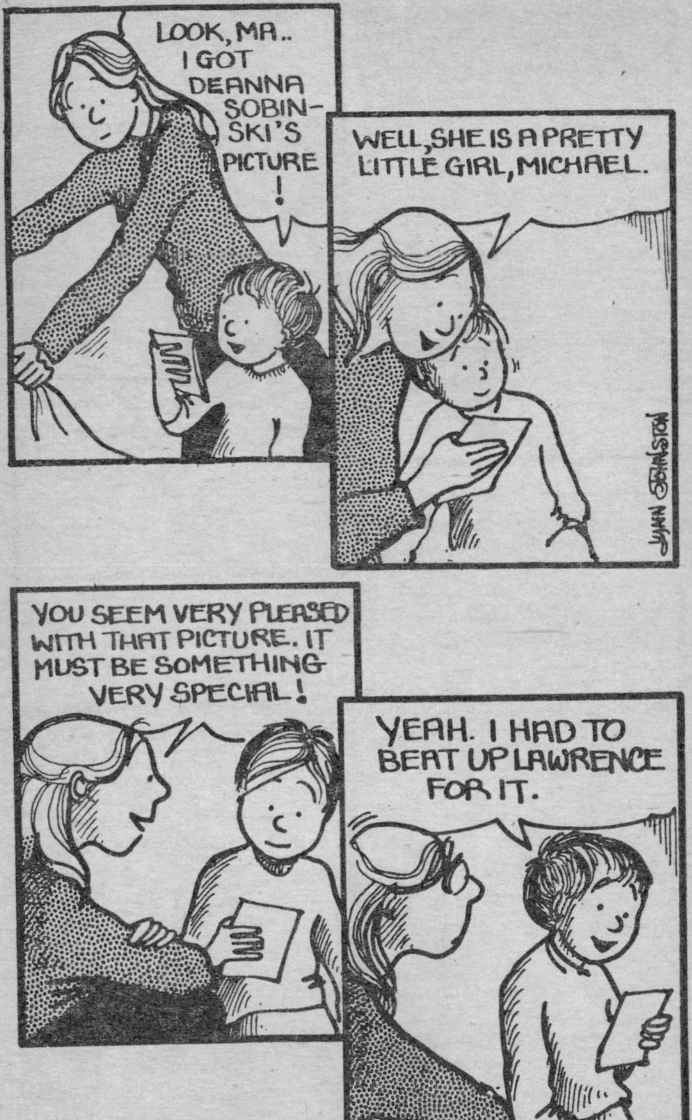
LOOK, MA.. I GOT DEANNA SOBIN-SKI'S PICTURE !
WELL, SHE IS A PRETTY LITTLE GIRL, MICHAEL.
LYNN JOHNSTON
YOU SEEM VERY PLEASED WITH THAT PICTURE. IT MUST BE SOMETHING VERY SPECIAL !
YEAH. I HAD TO BEAT UP LAWRENCE FOR IT.

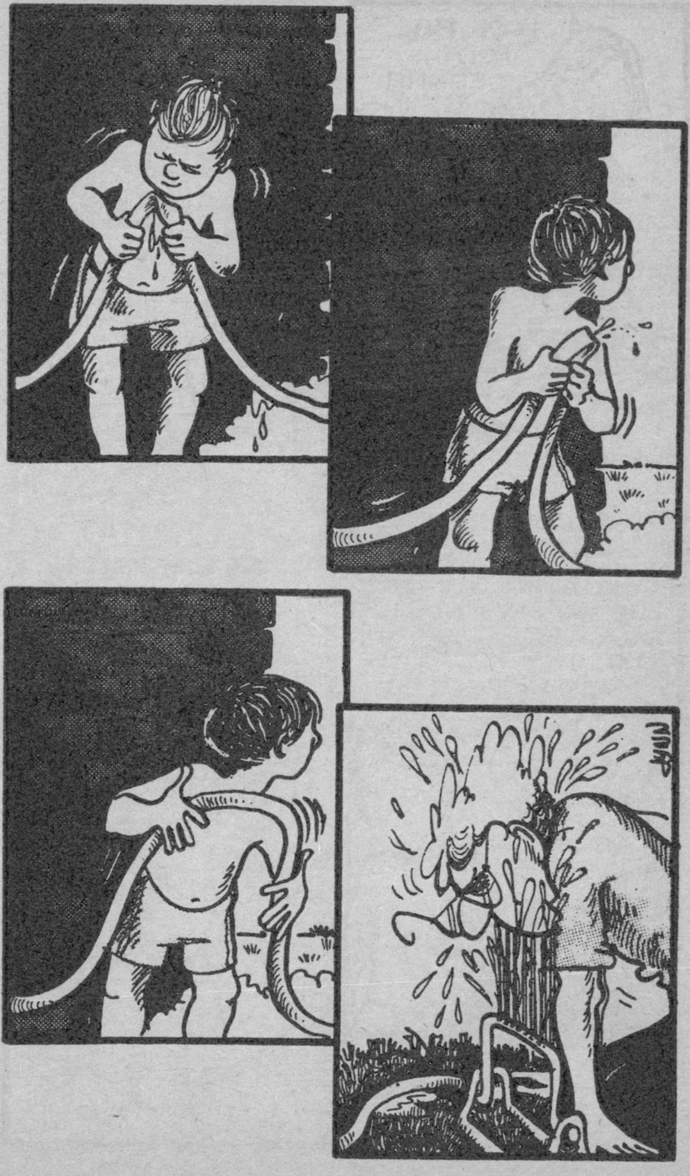

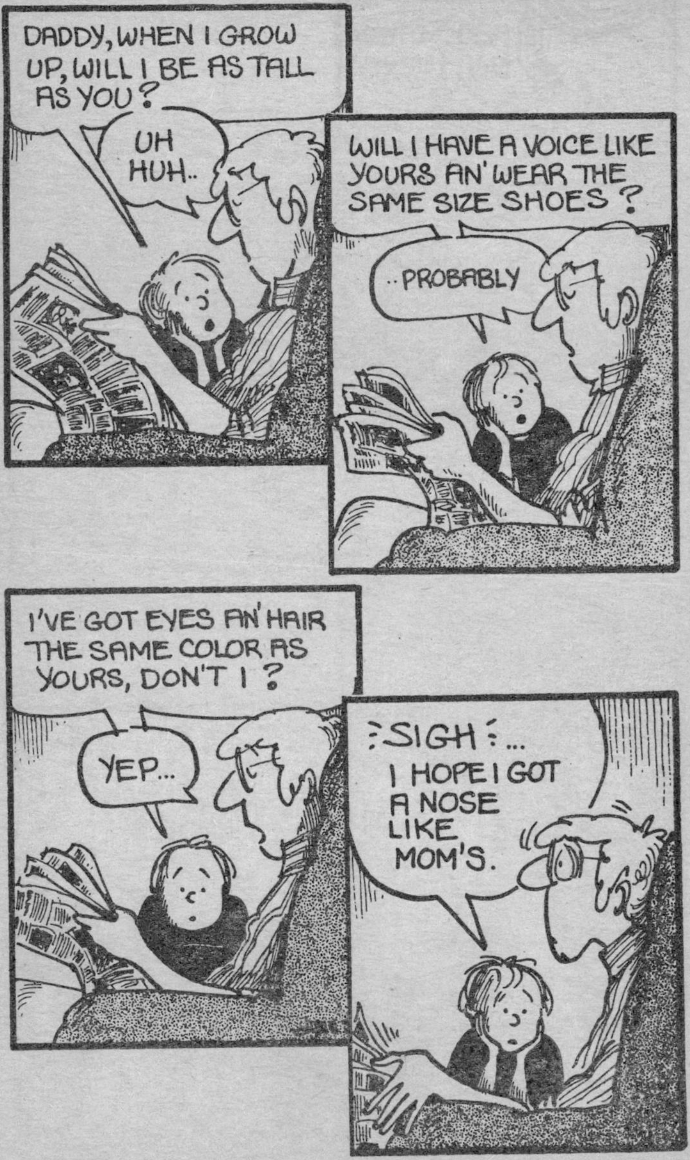
DADDY, WHEN I GROW UP, WILL I BE AS TALL AS YOU?
UH HUH..
WILL I HAVE A VOICE LIKE YOURS AN' WEAR THE SAME SIZE SHOES?
..PROBABLY
I'VE GOT EYES AN' HAIR THE SAME COLOR AS YOURS, DON'T I?
YEP...
SIGH ...
I HOPE I GOT A NOSE LIKE MOM'S.

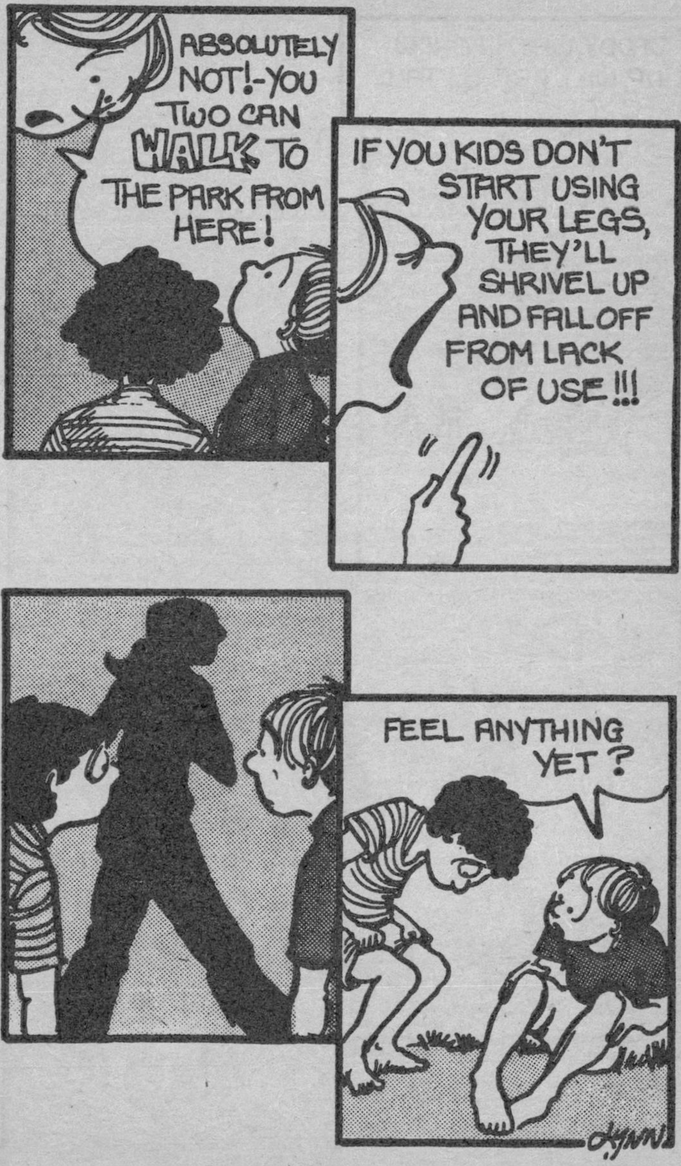
ABSOLUTELY NOT!-YOU TWO CAN WALK TO THE PARK FROM HERE!
IF YOU KIDS DON'T START USING YOUR LEGS, THEY'LL SHRIVEL UP AND FALL OFF FROM LACK OF USE!!!
FEEL ANYTHING YET?
Lynn

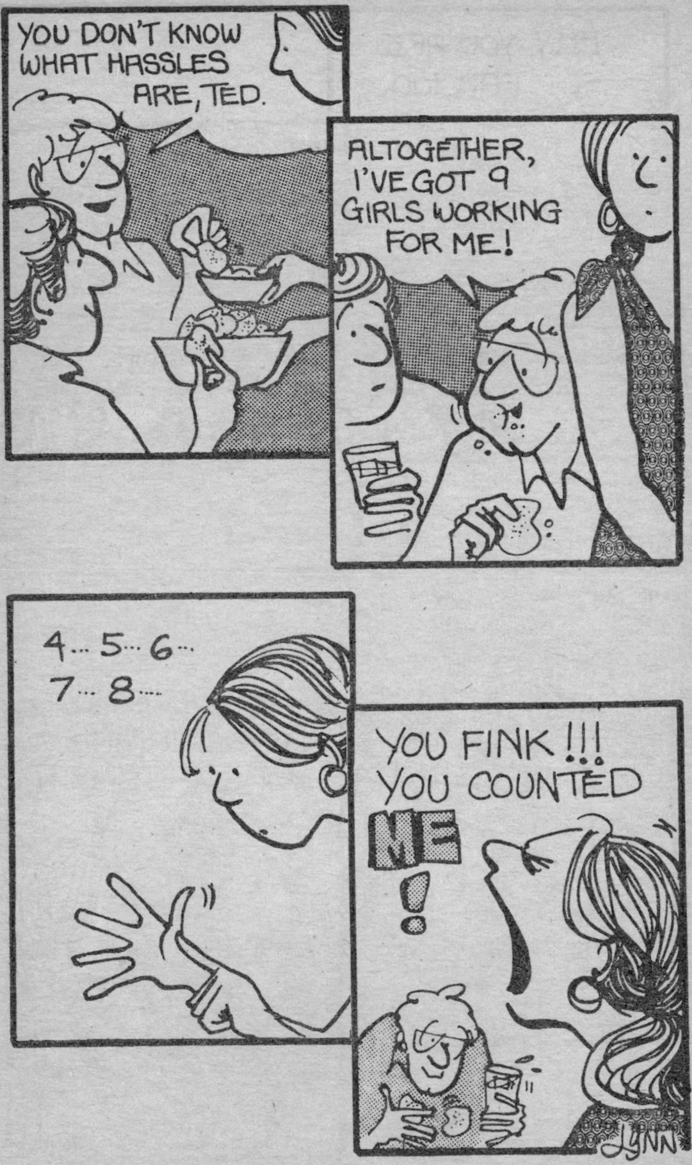
YOU DON'T KNOW WHAT HASSLES ARE, TED.
ALTOGETHER, I'VE GOT 9 GIRLS WORKING FOR ME!
4... 5... 6... 7... 8....
YOU FINK!!! YOU COUNTED ME!
LYNN

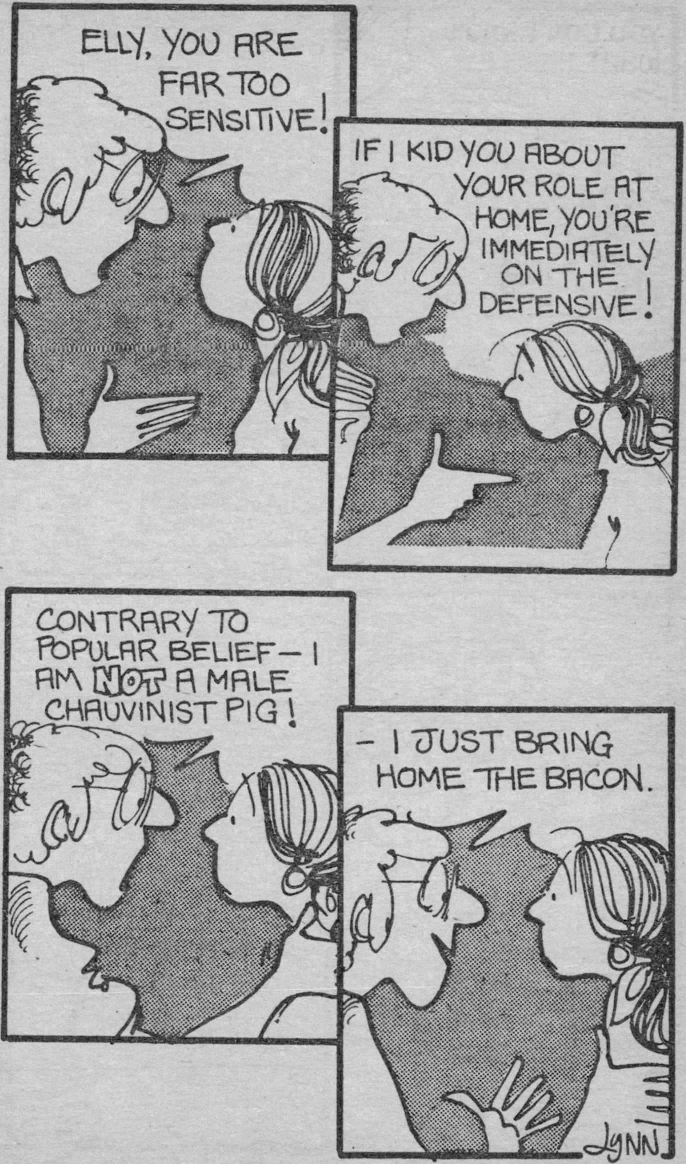
ELLY, YOU ARE FAR TOO SENSITIVE!
IF I KID YOU ABOUT YOUR ROLE AT HOME, YOU'RE IMMEDIATELY ON THE DEFENSIVE!
CONTRARY TO POPULAR BELIEF—I AM NOT A MALE CHAUVINIST PIG!
—I JUST BRING HOME THE BACON.
LYNN

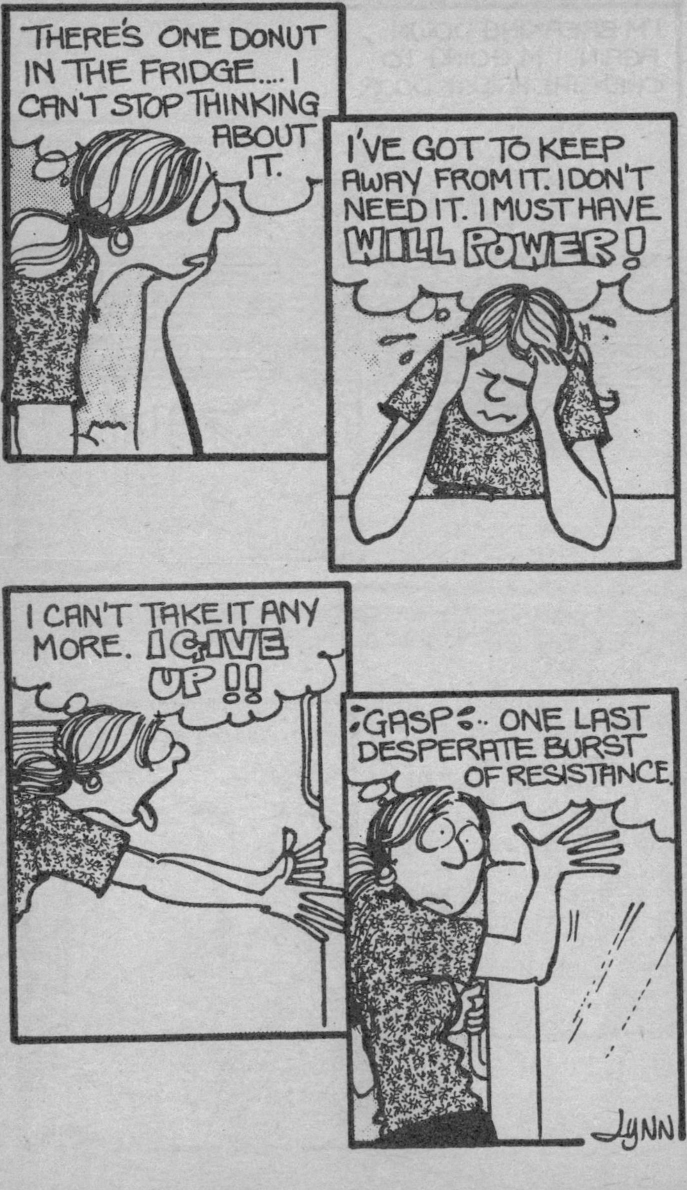
THERE'S ONE DONUT IN THE FRIDGE.... I CAN'T STOP THINKING ABOUT IT.
I'VE GOT TO KEEP AWAY FROM IT. I DON'T NEED IT. I MUST HAVE WILL POWER!
I CAN'T TAKE IT ANY MORE. I GIVE UP!!
GASP.. ONE LAST DESPERATE BURST OF RESISTANCE.
LYNN

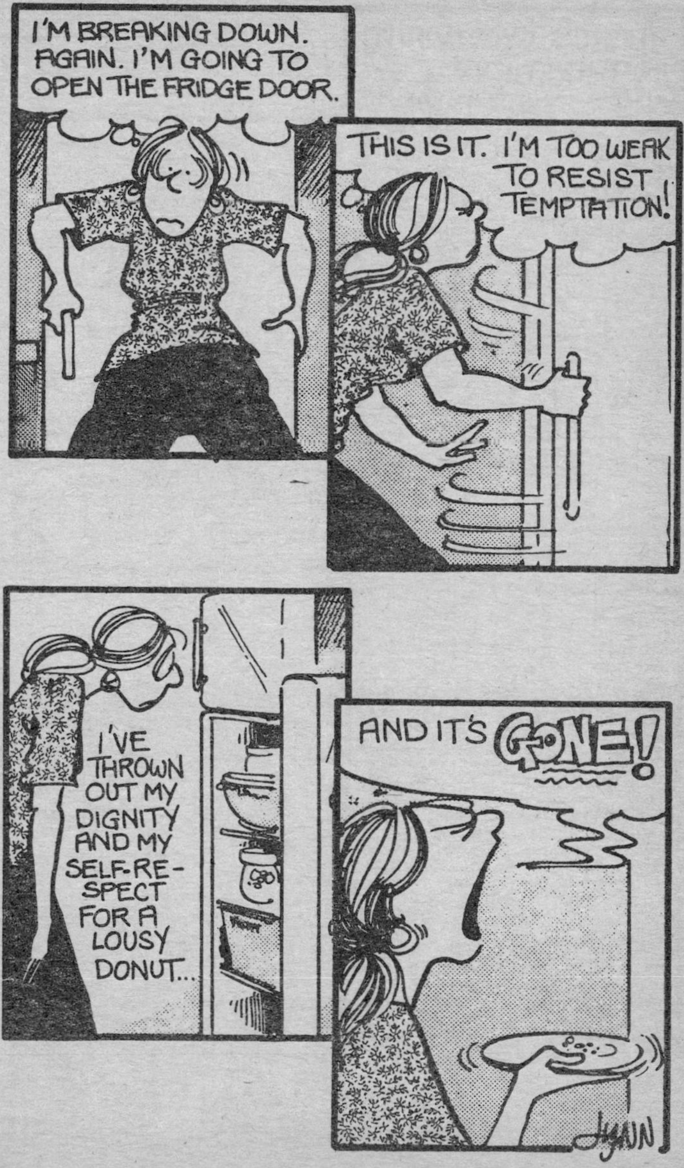
I'M BREAKING DOWN. AGAIN. I'M GOING TO OPEN THE FRIDGE DOOR.
THIS IS IT. I'M TOO WEAK TO RESIST TEMPTATION!
I'VE THROWN OUT MY DIGNITY AND MY SELF-RESPECT FOR A LOUSY DONUT...
AND IT'S GONE!

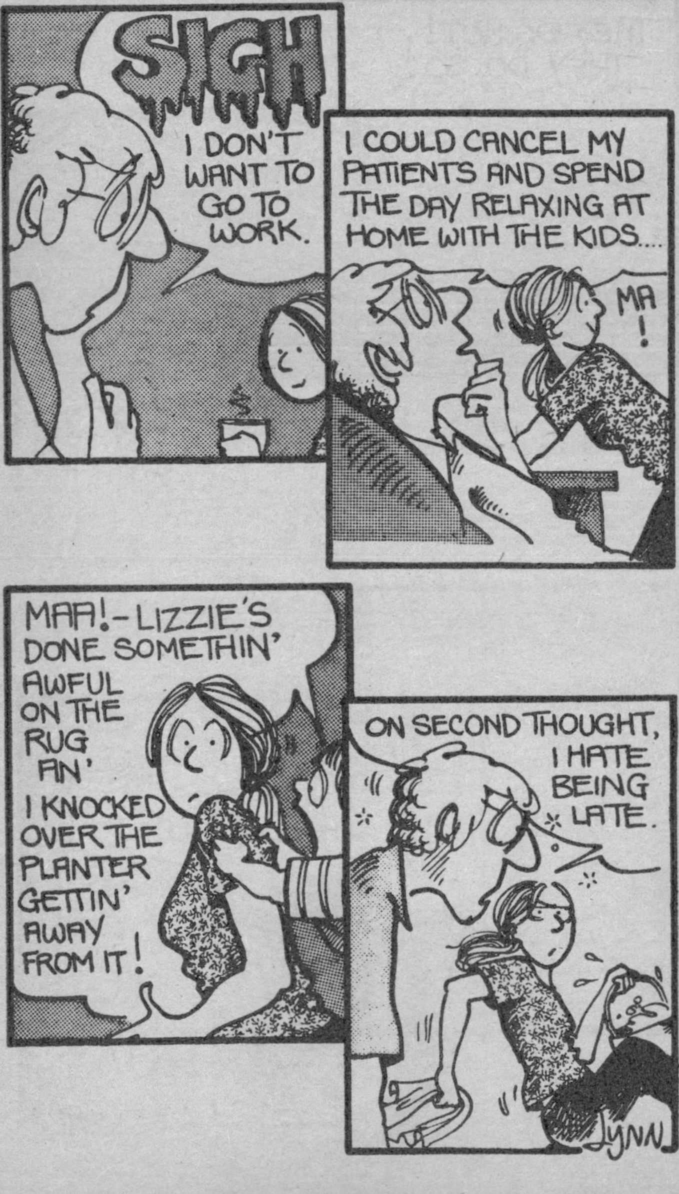
SIGH
I DON'T WANT TO GO TO WORK.
I COULD CANCEL MY PATIENTS AND SPEND THE DAY RELAXING AT HOME WITH THE KIDS....
MA!
MAA!-LIZZIE'S DONE SOMETHIN' AWFUL ON THE RUG AN' I KNOCKED OVER THE PLANTER GETTIN' AWAY FROM IT!
ON SECOND THOUGHT, I HATE BEING LATE.
LYNN

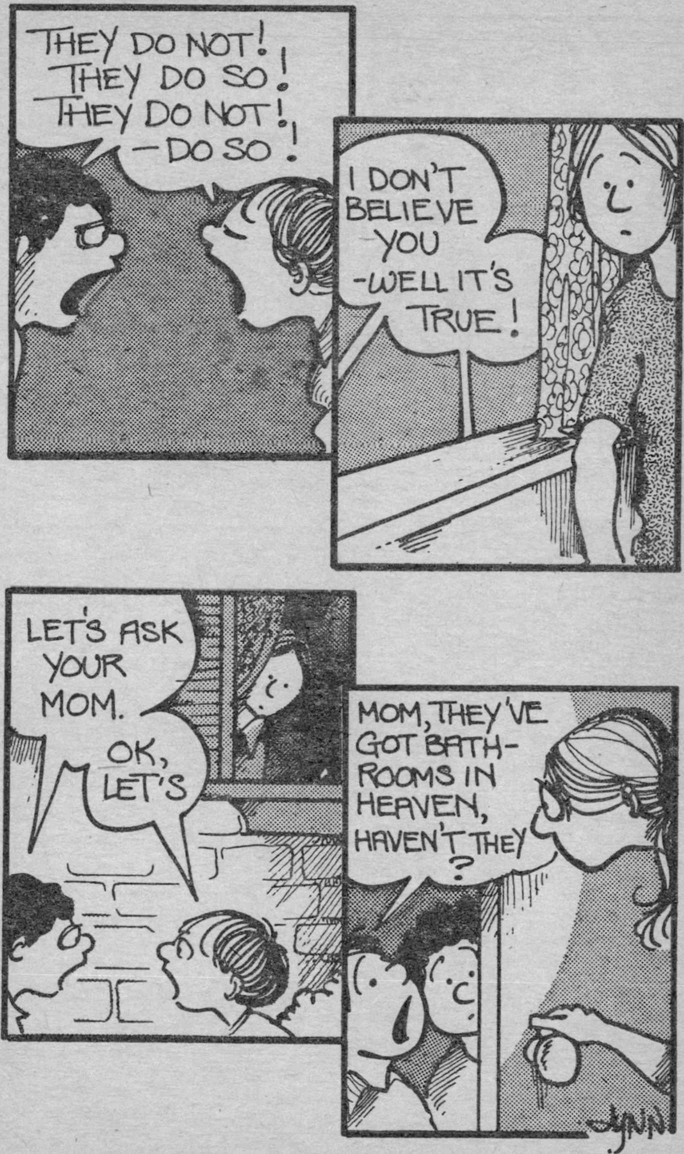
THEY DO NOT! THEY DO SO! THEY DO NOT! -DO SO!
I DON'T BELIEVE YOU -WELL IT'S TRUE!
LET'S ASK YOUR MOM.
OK, LET'S
MOM, THEY'VE GOT BATH-ROOMS IN HEAVEN, HAVEN'T THEY?
LYNN

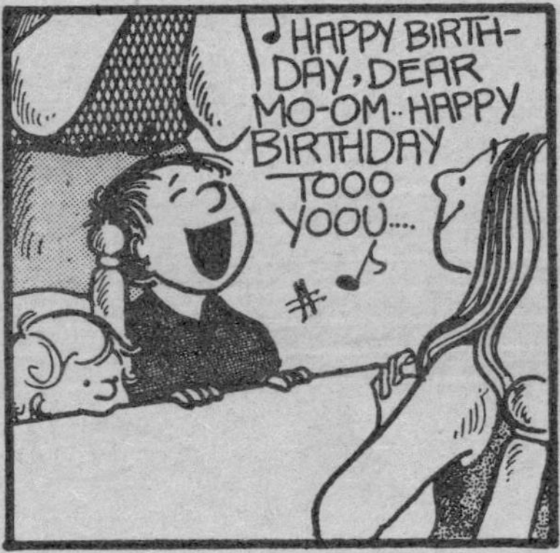
HAPPY BIRTH-DAY, DEAR MO-OM.. HAPPY BIRTHDAY TOOO YOOU....

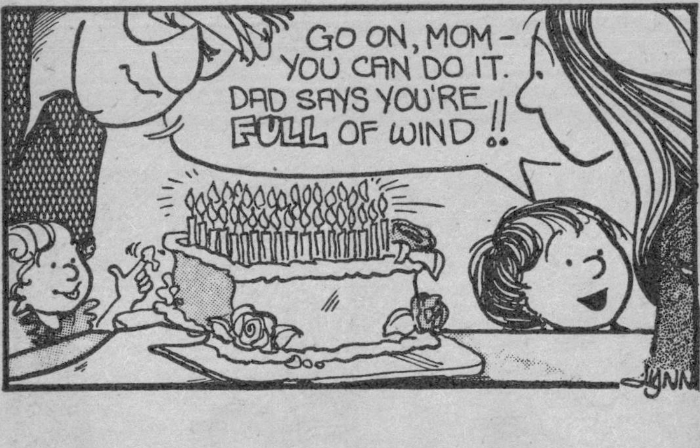
GO ON, MOM - YOU CAN DO IT. DAD SAYS YOU'RE FULL OF WIND !!
LYNN

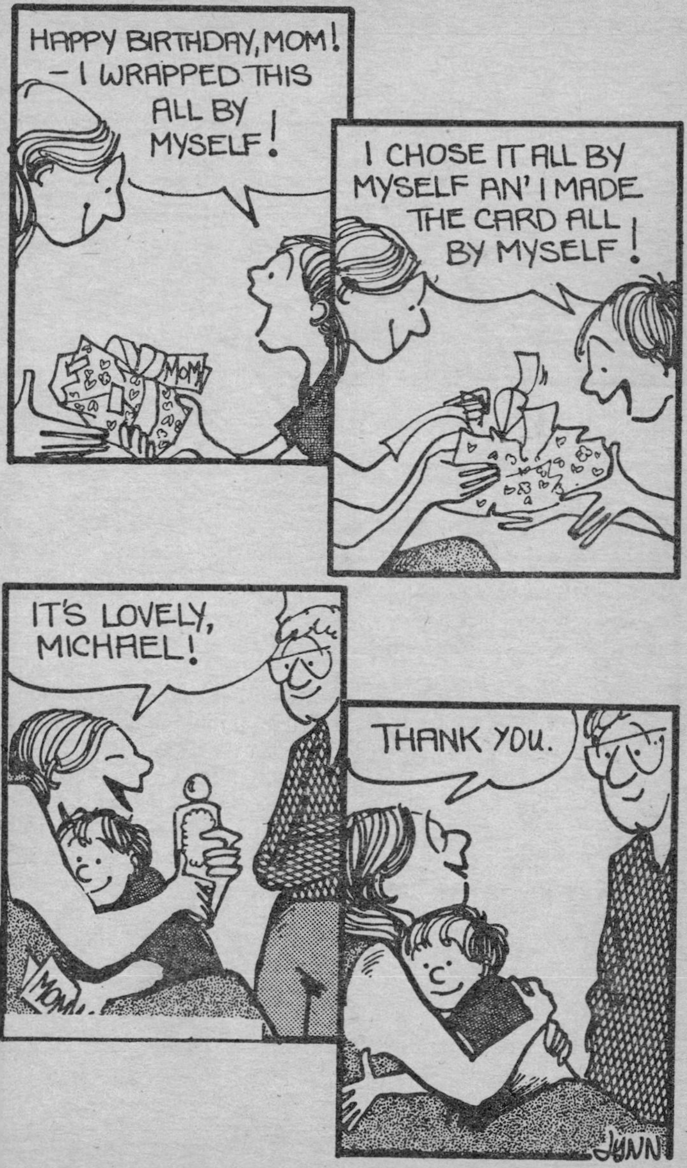
HAPPY BIRTHDAY, MOM! - I WRAPPED THIS ALL BY MYSELF!
MOM
I CHOSE IT ALL BY MYSELF AN' I MADE THE CARD ALL BY MYSELF!
IT'S LOVELY, MICHAEL!
THANK YOU.
LYNN

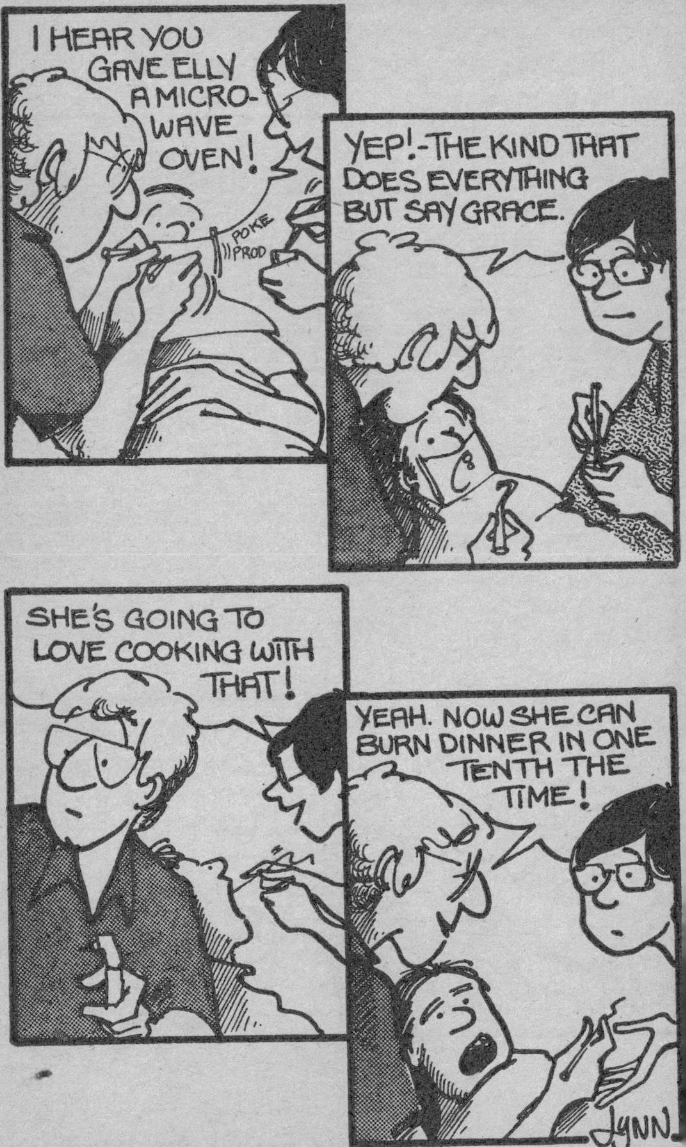
I HEAR YOU GAVE ELLY A MICRO-WAVE OVEN!
POKE
PROD
YEP!-THE KIND THAT DOES EVERYTHING BUT SAY GRACE.
SHE'S GOING TO LOVE COOKING WITH THAT!
YEAH. NOW SHE CAN BURN DINNER IN ONE TENTH THE TIME!
LYNN

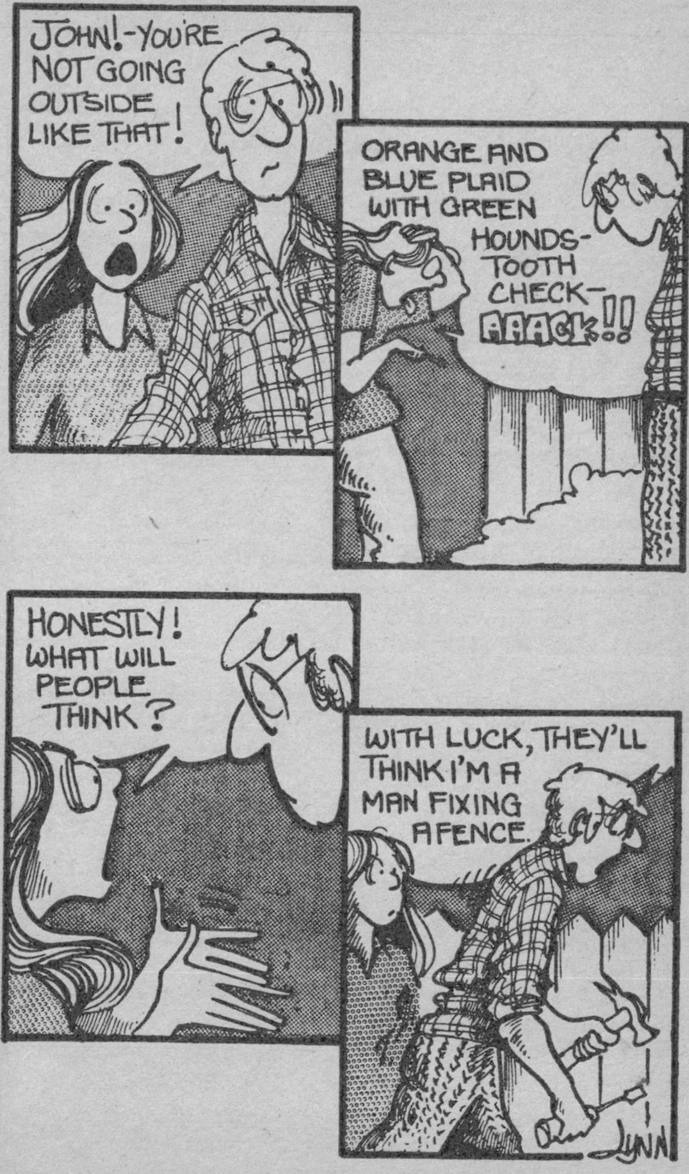
JOHN!-YOU'RE NOT GOING OUTSIDE LIKE THAT!
ORANGE AND BLUE PLAID WITH GREEN HOUNDS-TOOTH CHECK—AAACK!!
HONESTLY! WHAT WILL PEOPLE THINK?
WITH LUCK, THEY'LL THINK I'M A MAN FIXING A FENCE.
LYNN

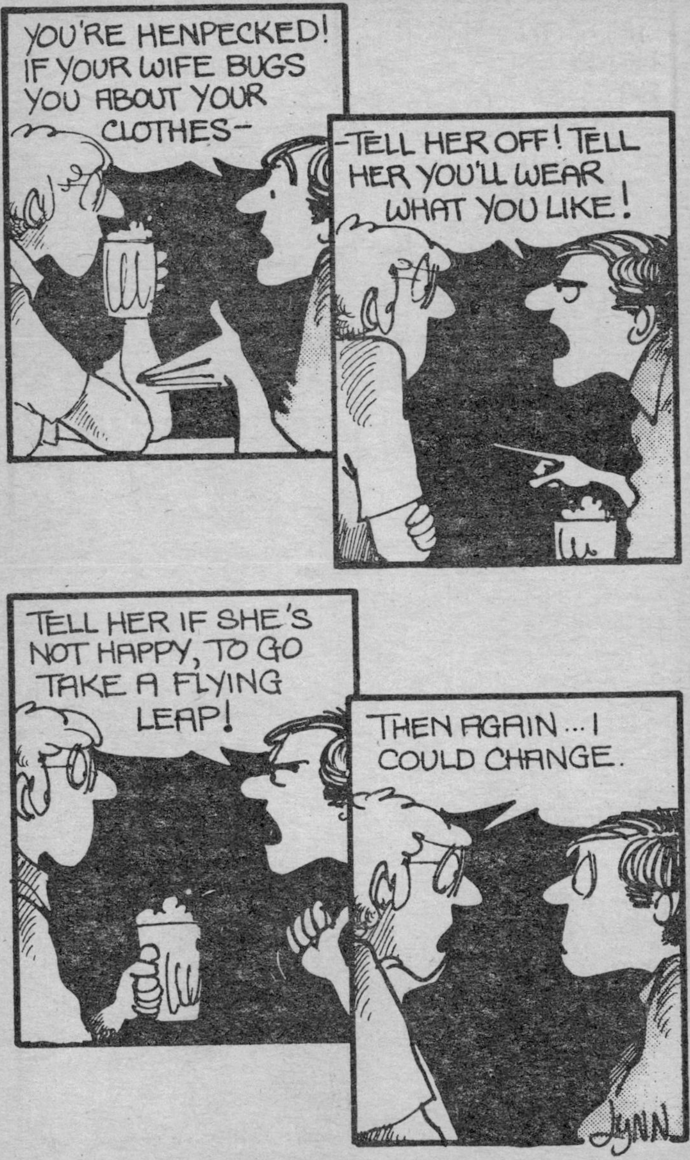
YOU'RE HENPECKED! IF YOUR WIFE BUGS YOU ABOUT YOUR CLOTHES-
-TELL HER OFF! TELL HER YOU'LL WEAR WHAT YOU LIKE!
TELL HER IF SHE'S NOT HAPPY, TO GO TAKE A FLYING LEAP!
THEN AGAIN ... I COULD CHANGE.
LYNN

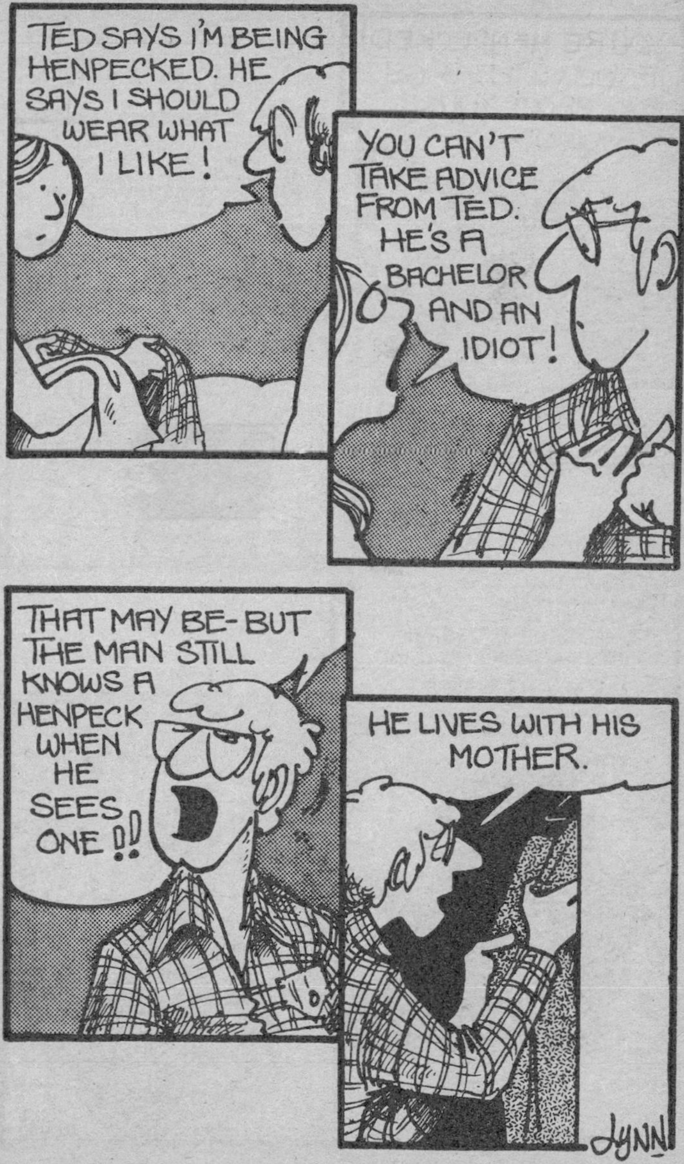
TED SAYS I'M BEING HENPECKED. HE SAYS I SHOULD WEAR WHAT I LIKE!
YOU CAN'T TAKE ADVICE FROM TED. HE'S A BACHELOR AND AN IDIOT!
THAT MAY BE- BUT THE MAN STILL KNOWS A HENPECK WHEN HE SEES ONE!!
HE LIVES WITH HIS MOTHER.
LYNN

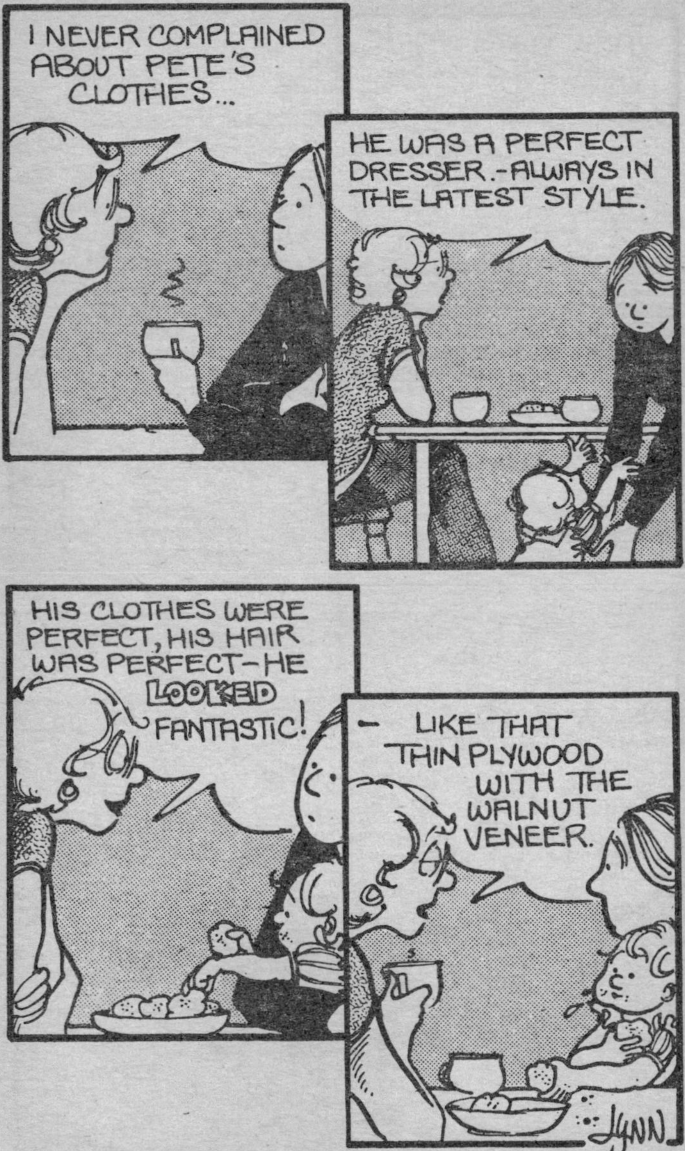
I NEVER COMPLAINED ABOUT PETE'S CLOTHES...
HE WAS A PERFECT DRESSER.-ALWAYS IN THE LATEST STYLE.
HIS CLOTHES WERE PERFECT, HIS HAIR WAS PERFECT-HE LOOKED FANTASTIC!
- LIKE THAT THIN PLYWOOD WITH THE WALNUT VENEER.
LYNN

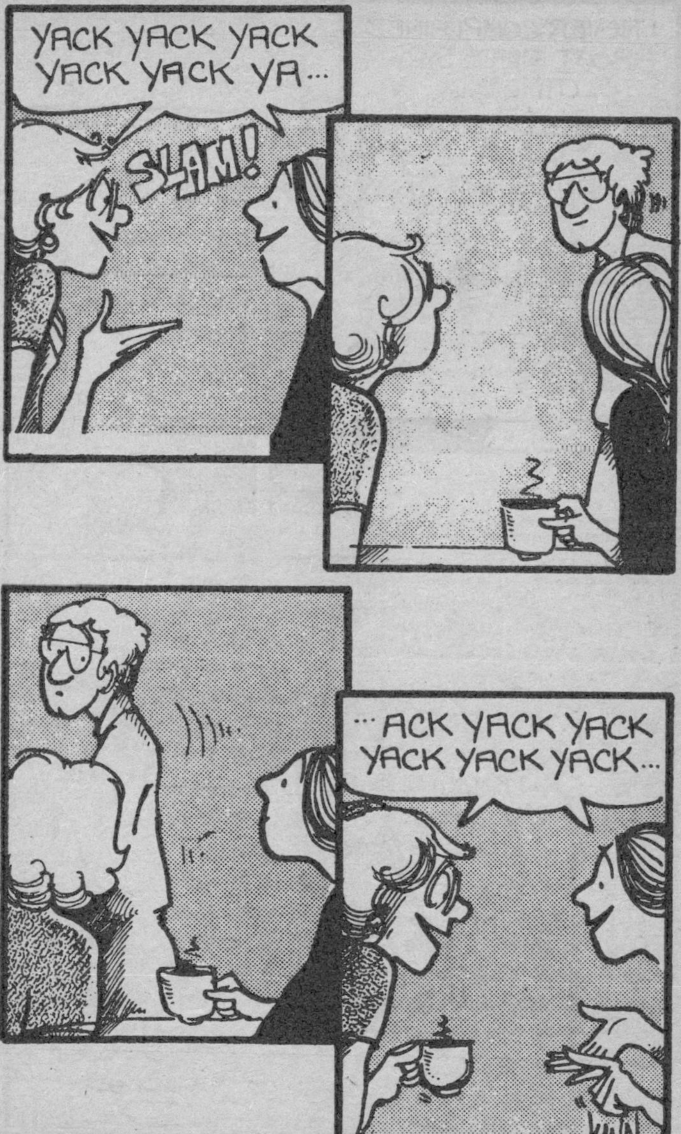
YACK YACK YACK
YACK YACK YA...
SLAM!
...ACK YACK YACK
YACK YACK YACK...
LYNN

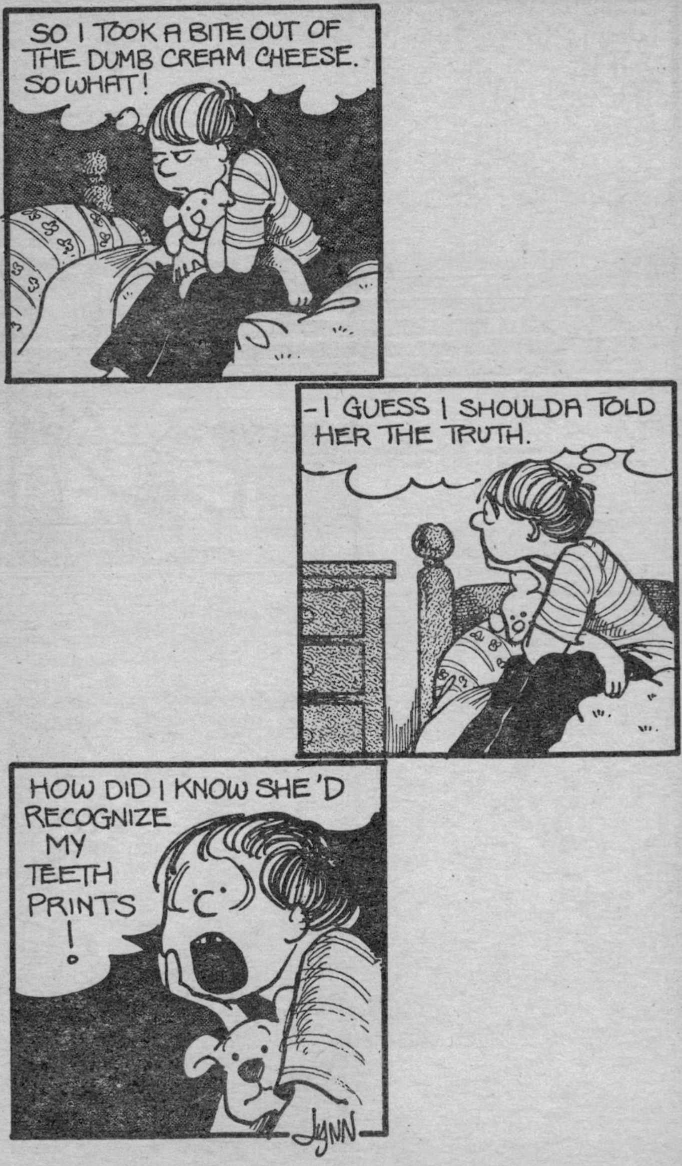
SO I TOOK A BITE OUT OF THE DUMB CREAM CHEESE. SO WHAT!
-I GUESS I SHOULDA TOLD HER THE TRUTH.
HOW DID I KNOW SHE'D RECOGNIZE MY TEETH PRINTS!
LYNN

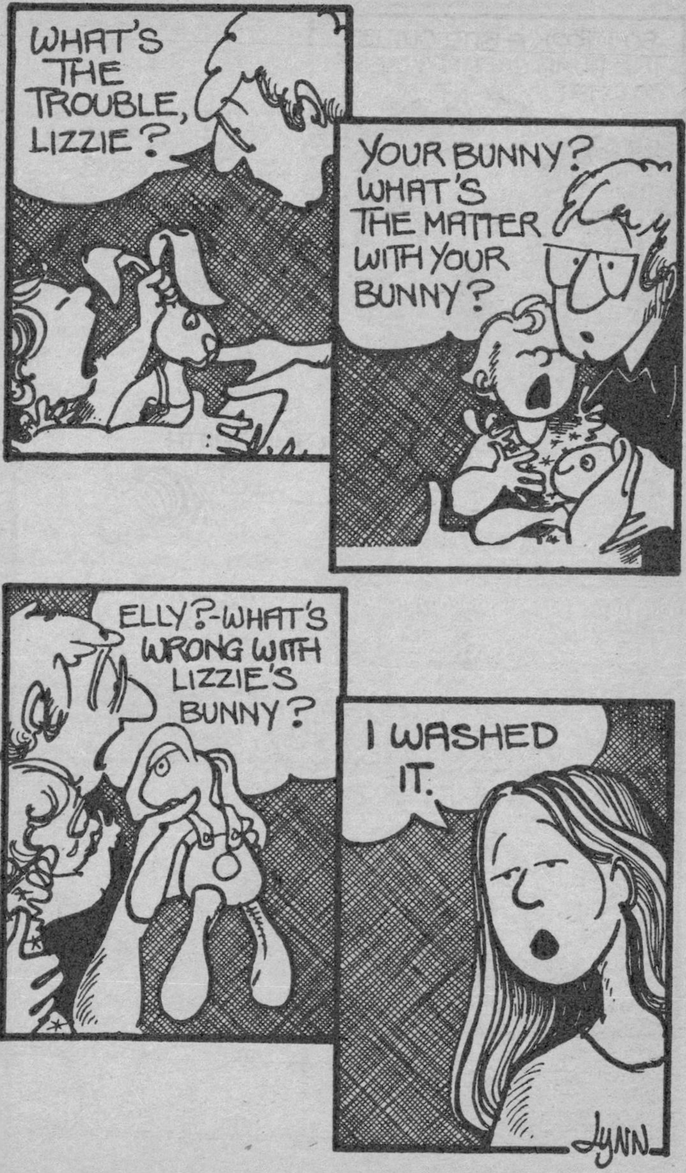
WHAT'S THE TROUBLE, LIZZIE?
YOUR BUNNY? WHAT'S THE MATTER WITH YOUR BUNNY?
ELLY?-WHAT'S WRONG WITH LIZZIE'S BUNNY?
I WASHED IT.
LYNN

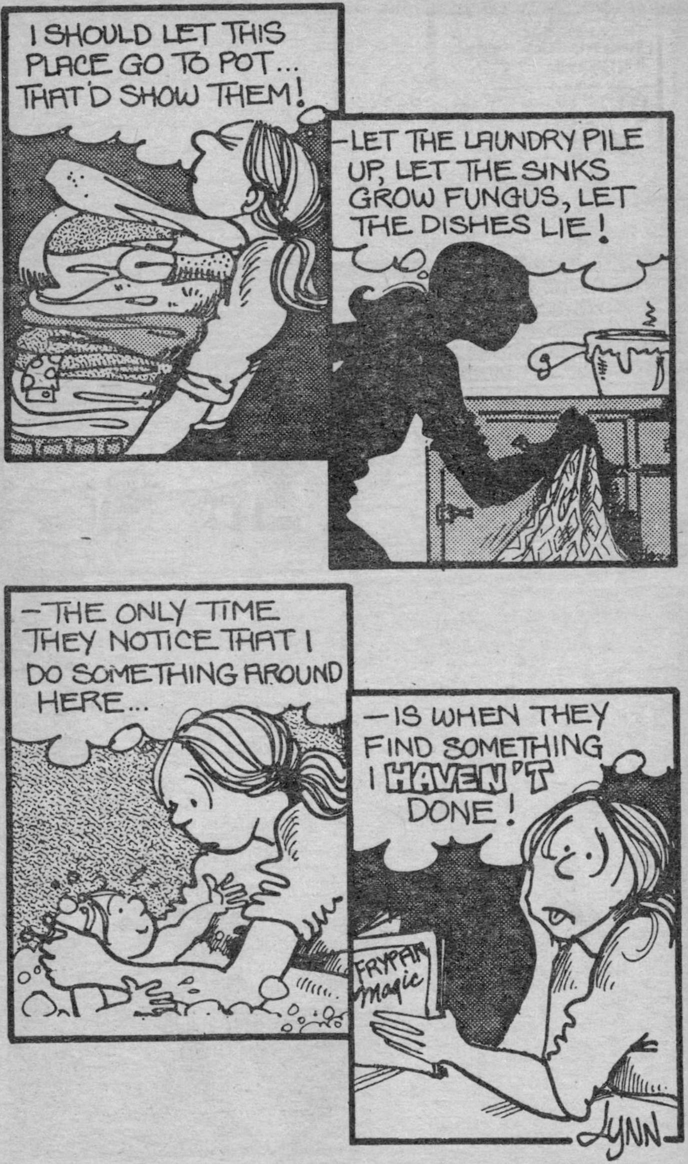
I SHOULD LET THIS PLACE GO TO POT... THAT'D SHOW THEM!
-LET THE LAUNDRY PILE UP, LET THE SINKS GROW FUNGUS, LET THE DISHES LIE!
-THE ONLY TIME THEY NOTICE THAT I DO SOMETHING AROUND HERE...
-IS WHEN THEY FIND SOMETHING I HAVEN'T DONE!
FRYPAN magic
LYNN

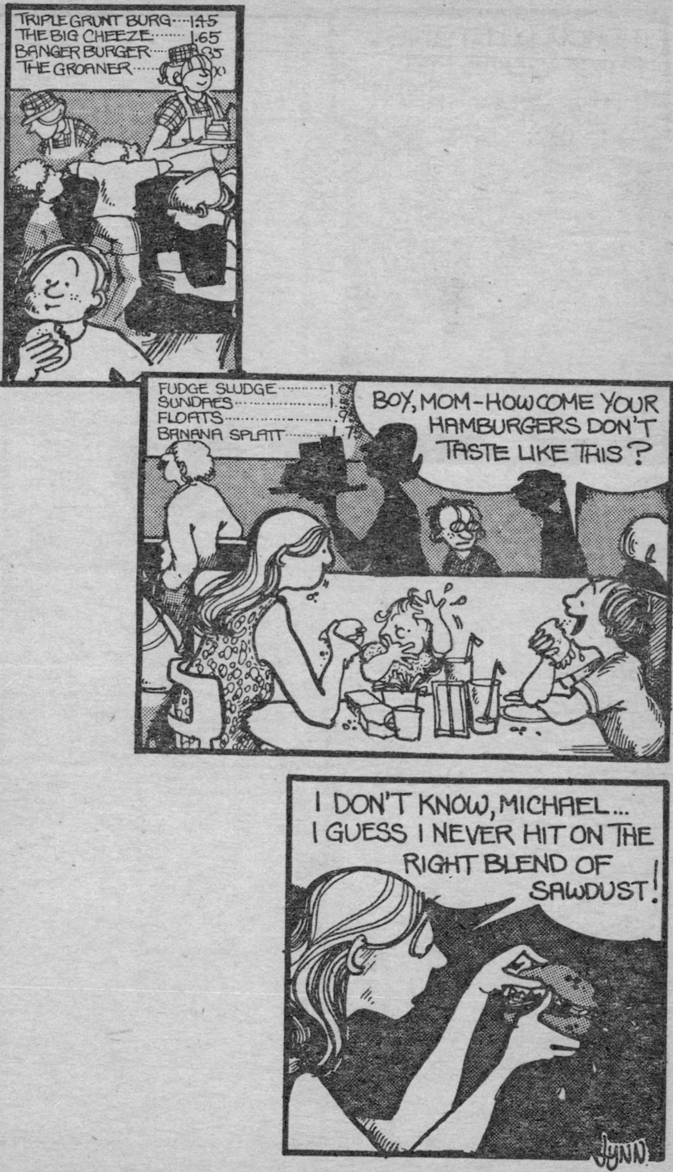
TRIPLE GRUNT BURG 1.45
THE BIG CHEEZE 1.65
BANGER BURGER
THE GROANER
FUDGE SLUDGE
SUNDAES
FLOATS
BANANA SPLATT
BOY, MOM - HOW COME YOUR HAMBURGERS DON'T TASTE LIKE THIS?
I DON'T KNOW, MICHAEL... I GUESS I NEVER HIT ON THE RIGHT BLEND OF SAWDUST!
LYNN

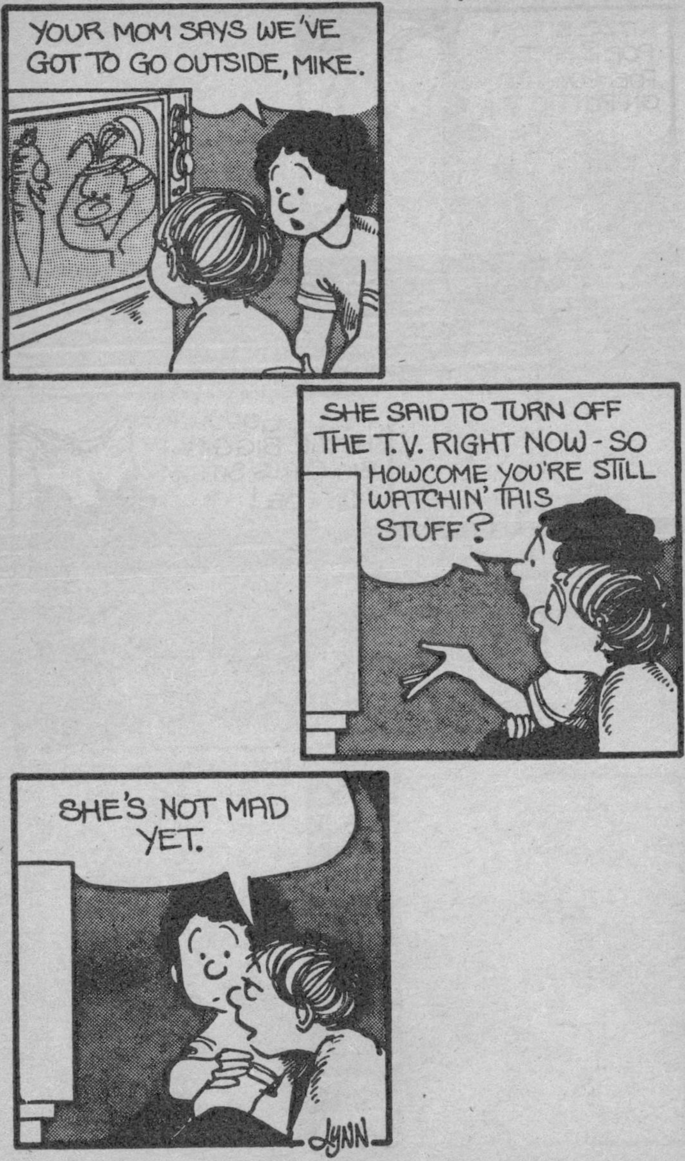
YOUR MOM SAYS WE'VE GOT TO GO OUTSIDE, MIKE.
SHE SAID TO TURN OFF THE T.V. RIGHT NOW - SO HOWCOME YOU'RE STILL WATCHIN' THIS STUFF?
SHE'S NOT MAD YET.
LYNN

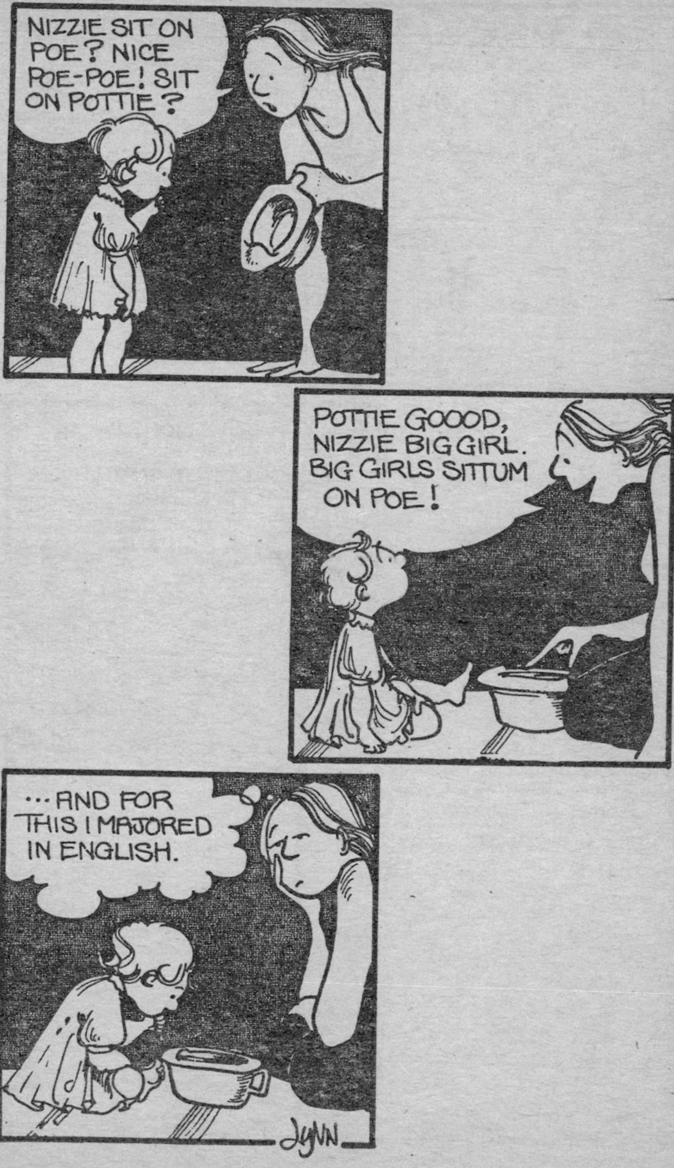
NIZZIE SIT ON POE? NICE POE-POE! SIT ON POTTIE?
POTTIE GOOOD, NIZZIE BIG GIRL. BIG GIRLS SITTUM ON POE!
...AND FOR THIS I MAJORED IN ENGLISH.
LYNN

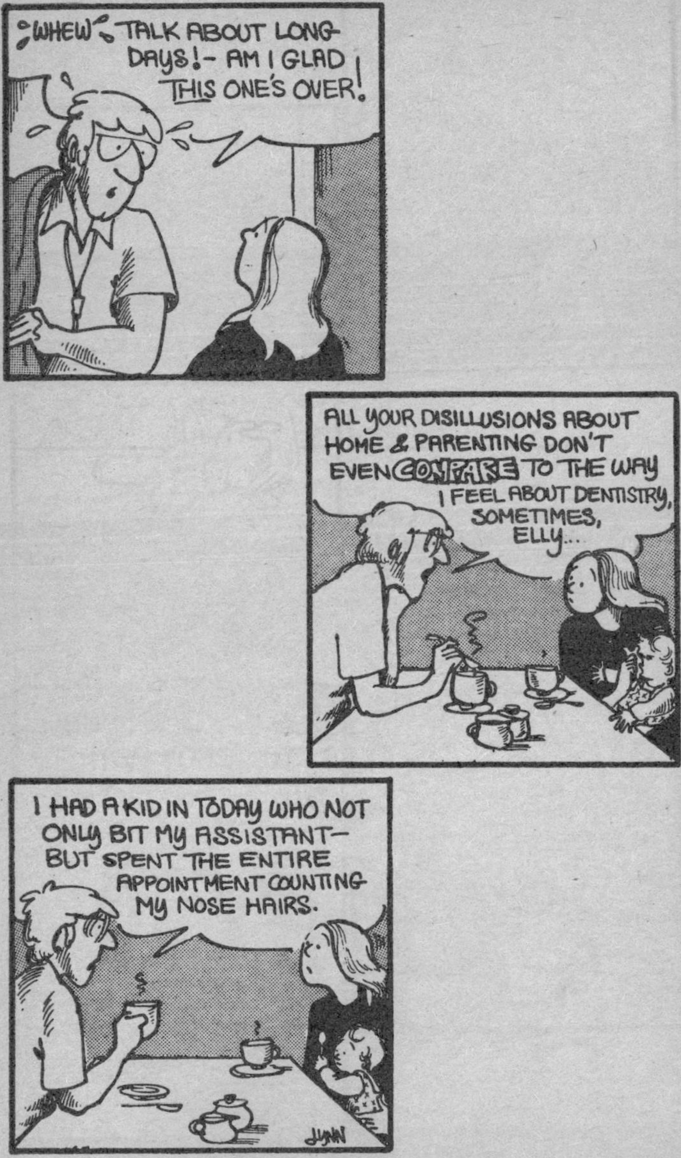
WHEW - TALK ABOUT LONG DAYS! - AM I GLAD THIS ONE'S OVER!
ALL YOUR DISILLUSIONS ABOUT HOME & PARENTING DON'T EVEN COMPARE TO THE WAY I FEEL ABOUT DENTISTRY, SOMETIMES, ELLY...
I HAD A KID IN TODAY WHO NOT ONLY BIT MY ASSISTANT- BUT SPENT THE ENTIRE APPOINTMENT COUNTING MY NOSE HAIRS.
LYNN

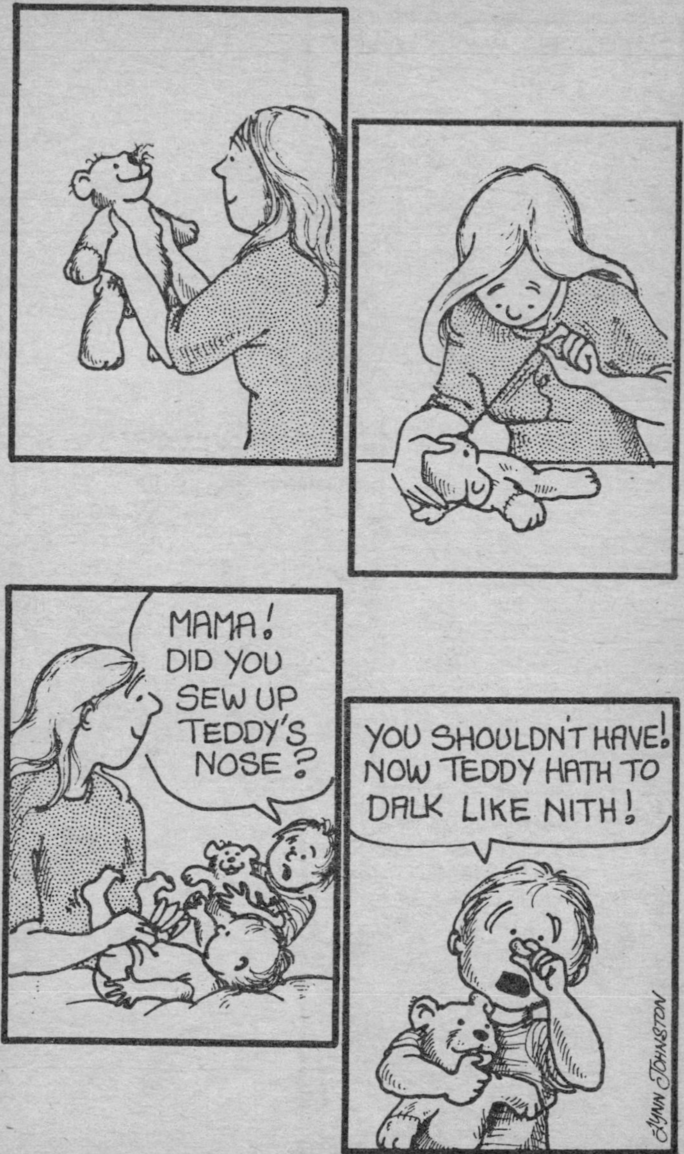
MAMA! DID YOU SEW UP TEDDY'S NOSE?
YOU SHOULDN'T HAVE! NOW TEDDY HATH TO DALK LIKE NITH!
LYNN JOHNSTON

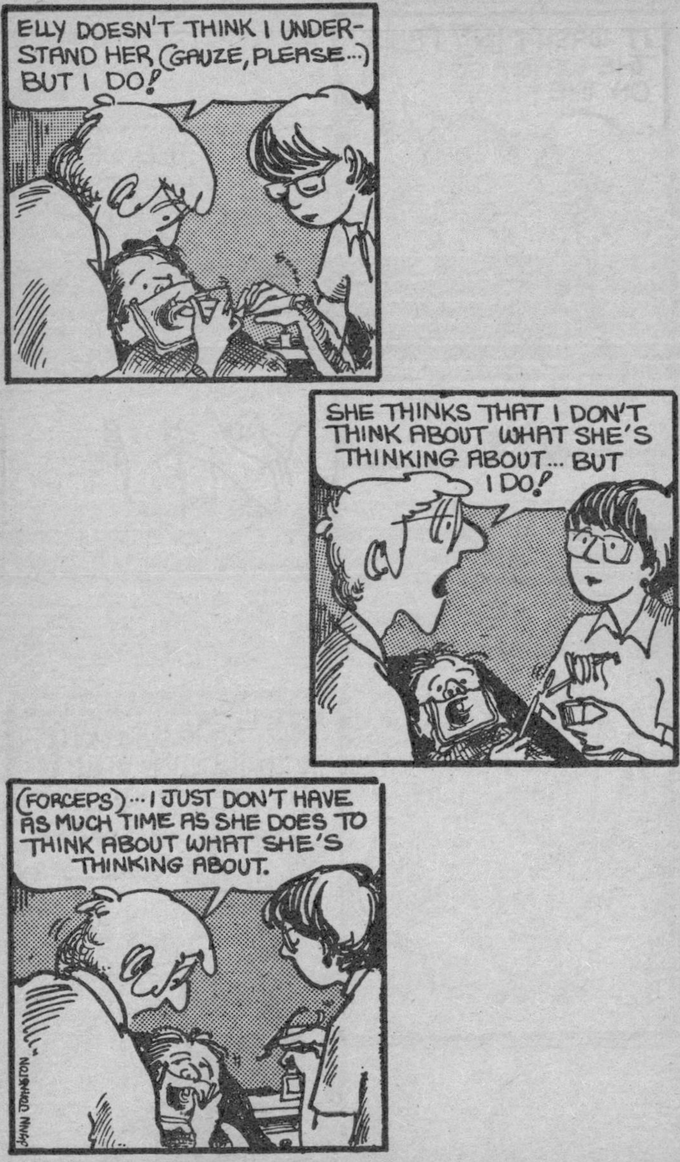
ELLY DOESN'T THINK I UNDERSTAND HER (GAUZE, PLEASE...) BUT I DO!
SHE THINKS THAT I DON'T THINK ABOUT WHAT SHE'S THINKING ABOUT... BUT I DO!
(FORCEPS)... I JUST DON'T HAVE AS MUCH TIME AS SHE DOES TO THINK ABOUT WHAT SHE'S THINKING ABOUT.
LYNN JOHNSTON

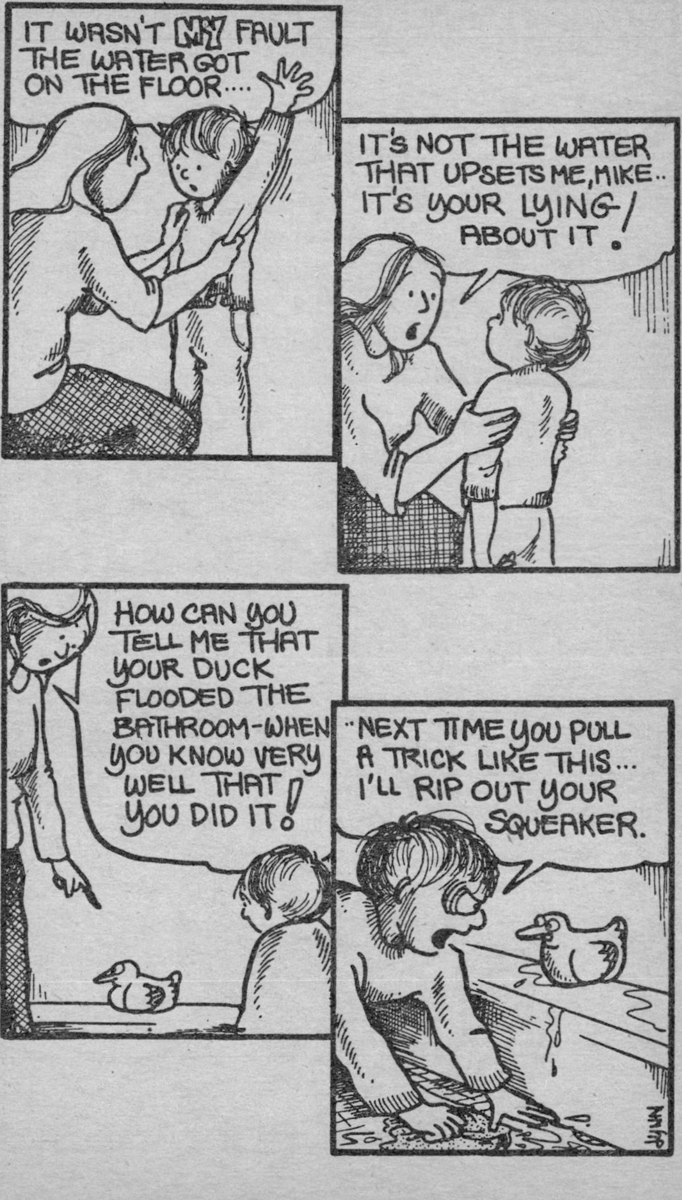
IT WASN'T MY FAULT THE WATER GOT ON THE FLOOR....
IT'S NOT THE WATER THAT UPSETS ME, MIKE.. IT'S YOUR LYING ABOUT IT!
HOW CAN YOU TELL ME THAT YOUR DUCK FLOODED THE BATHROOM-WHEN YOU KNOW VERY WELL THAT YOU DID IT!
..NEXT TIME YOU PULL A TRICK LIKE THIS... I'LL RIP OUT YOUR SQUEAKER.

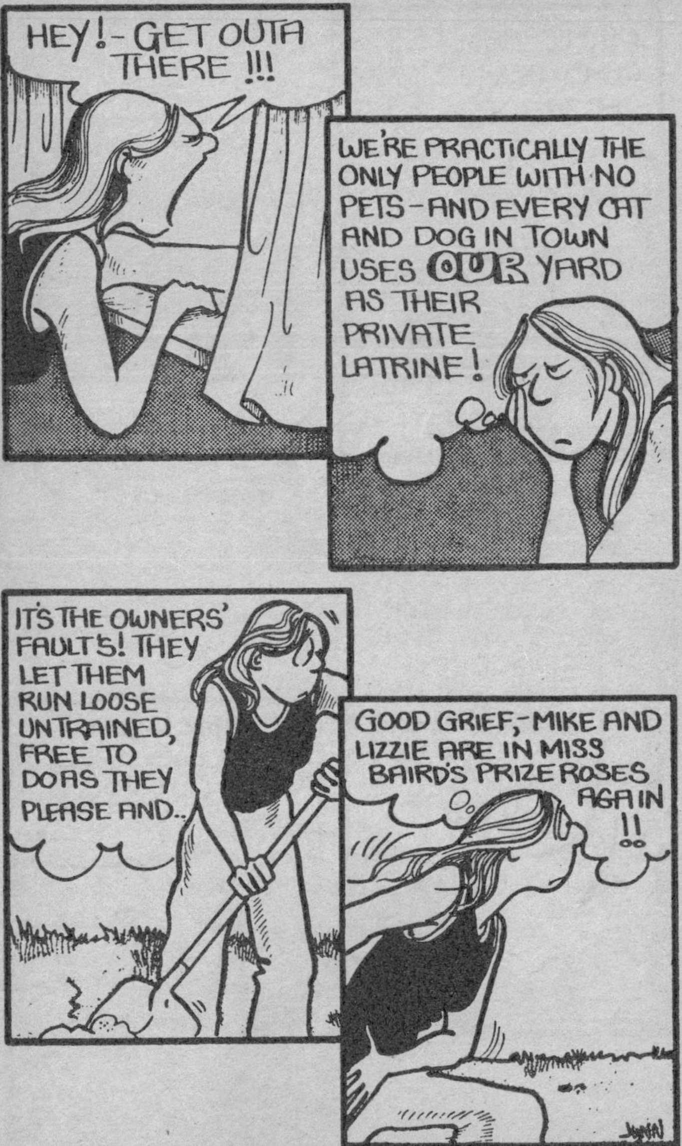
HEY!- GET OUTA THERE !!!
WE'RE PRACTICALLY THE ONLY PEOPLE WITH NO PETS - AND EVERY CAT AND DOG IN TOWN USES OUR YARD AS THEIR PRIVATE LATRINE!
IT'S THE OWNERS' FAULT'S! THEY LET THEM RUN LOOSE UNTRAINED, FREE TO DO AS THEY PLEASE AND..
GOOD GRIEF,- MIKE AND LIZZIE ARE IN MISS BAIRD'S PRIZE ROSES AGAIN !!

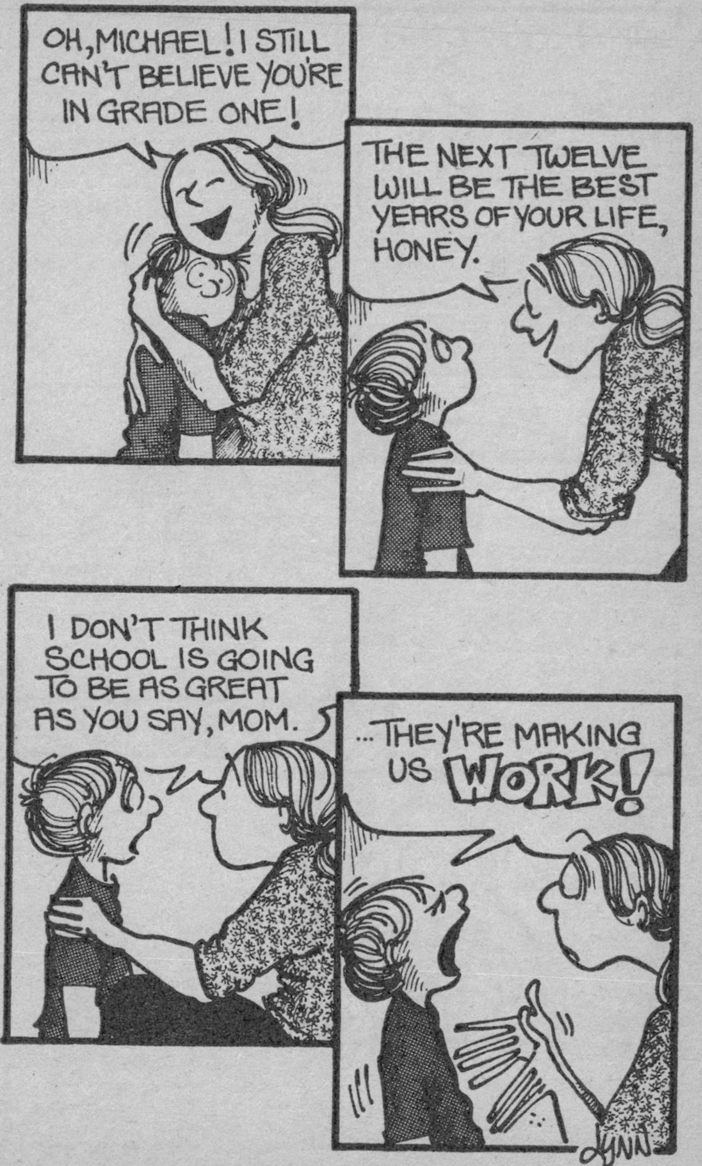
OH, MICHAEL! I STILL CAN'T BELIEVE YOU'RE IN GRADE ONE!
THE NEXT TWELVE WILL BE THE BEST YEARS OF YOUR LIFE, HONEY.
I DON'T THINK SCHOOL IS GOING TO BE AS GREAT AS YOU SAY, MOM.
...THEY'RE MAKING US WORK!
LYNN

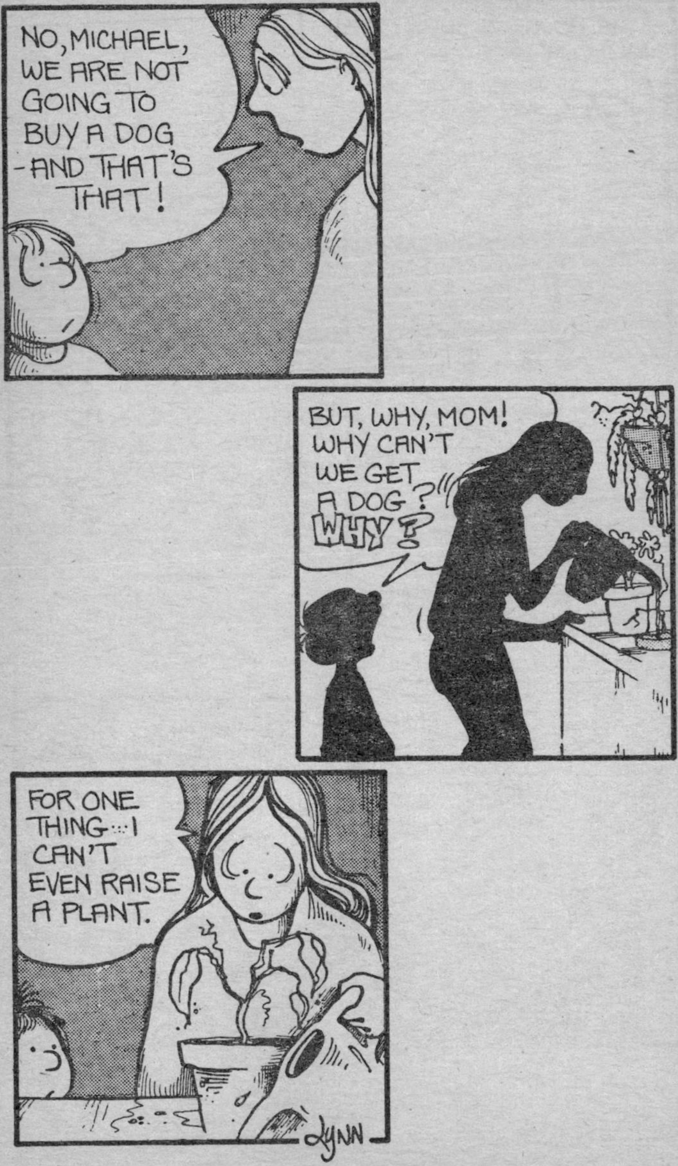
NO, MICHAEL, WE ARE NOT GOING TO BUY A DOG - AND THAT'S THAT!
BUT, WHY, MOM! WHY CAN'T WE GET A DOG? WHY?
FOR ONE THING... I CAN'T EVEN RAISE A PLANT.
LYNN

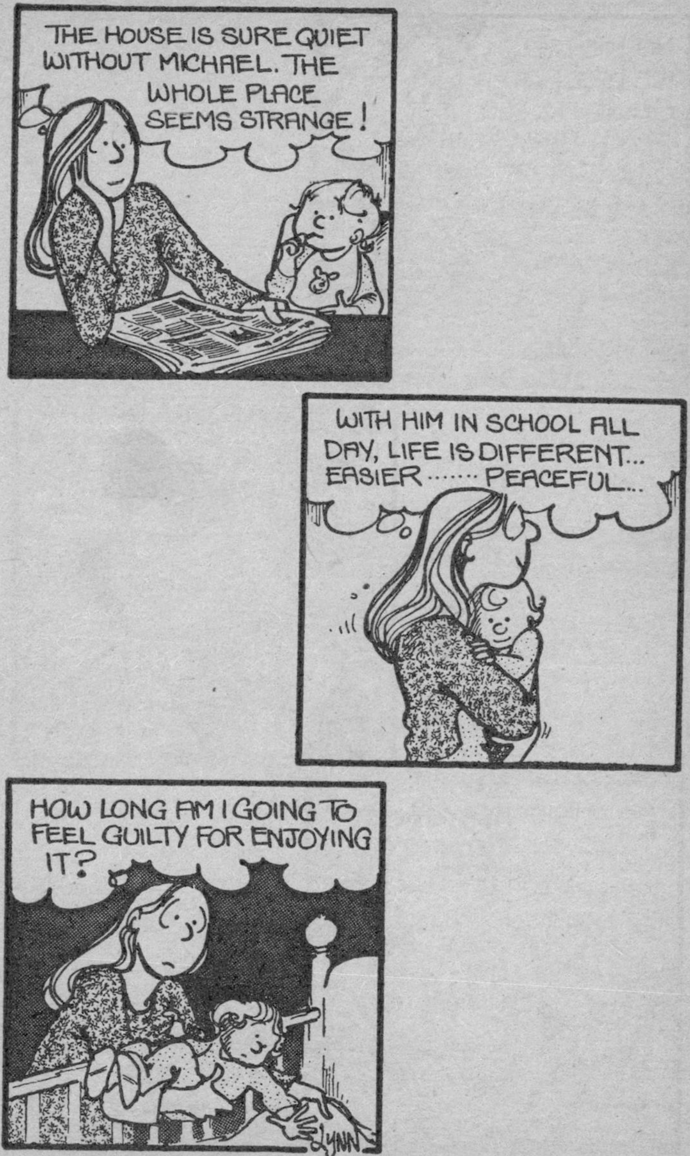
THE HOUSE IS SURE QUIET WITHOUT MICHAEL. THE WHOLE PLACE SEEMS STRANGE!
WITH HIM IN SCHOOL ALL DAY, LIFE IS DIFFERENT... EASIER .... PEACEFUL...
HOW LONG AM I GOING TO FEEL GUILTY FOR ENJOYING IT?
LYNN

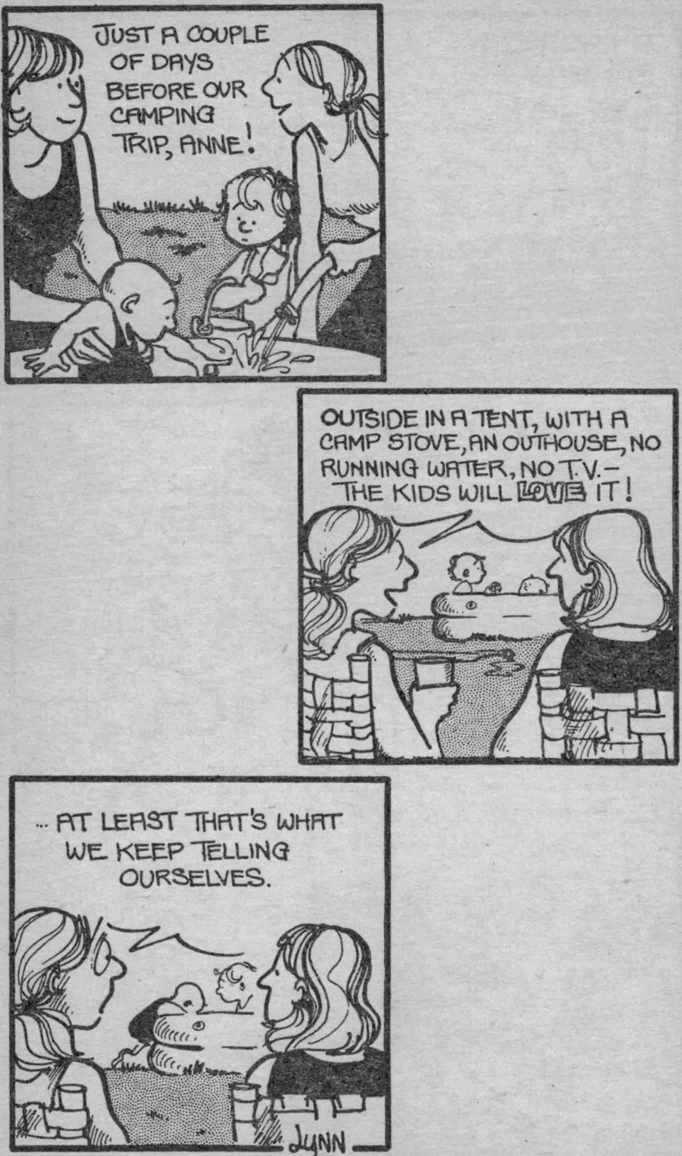
JUST A COUPLE OF DAYS BEFORE OUR CAMPING TRIP, ANNE!
OUTSIDE IN A TENT, WITH A CAMP STOVE, AN OUTHOUSE, NO RUNNING WATER, NO T.V. – THE KIDS WILL LOVE IT!
... AT LEAST THAT'S WHAT WE KEEP TELLING OURSELVES.
LYNN

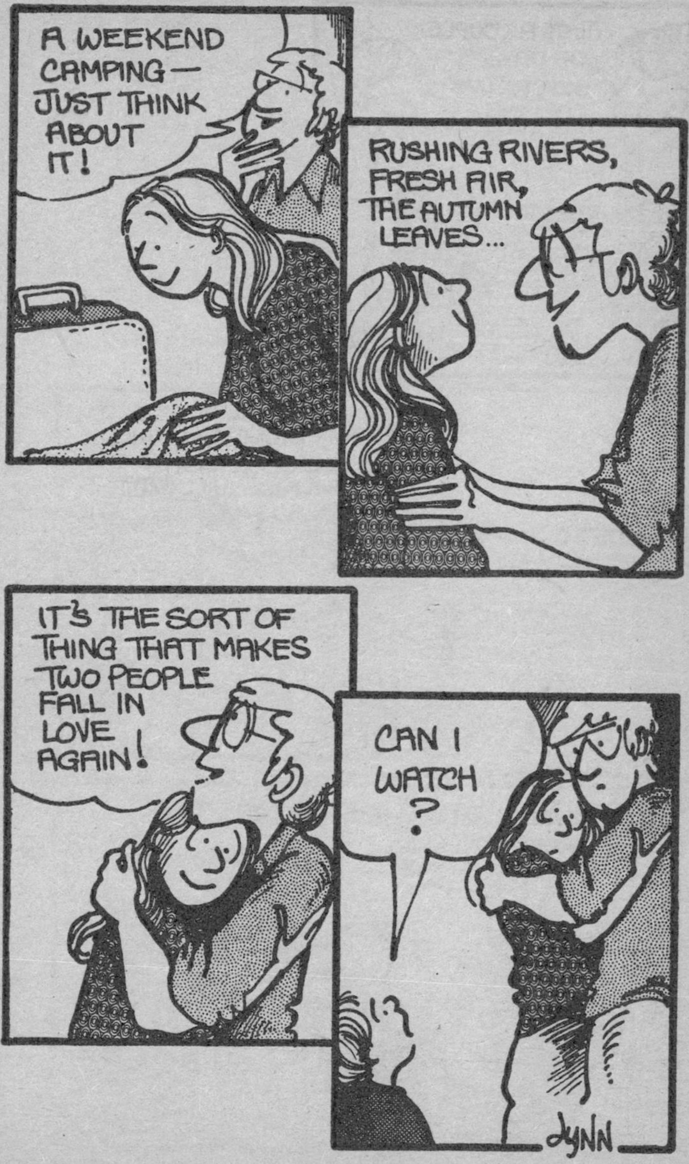
A WEEKEND CAMPING— JUST THINK ABOUT IT!
RUSHING RIVERS, FRESH AIR, THE AUTUMN LEAVES...
IT'S THE SORT OF THING THAT MAKES TWO PEOPLE FALL IN LOVE AGAIN!
CAN I WATCH?
LYNN

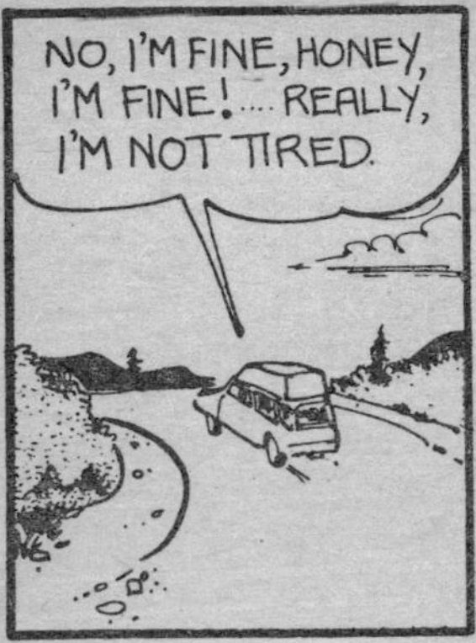
NO, I'M FINE, HONEY, I'M FINE!.... REALLY, I'M NOT TIRED.

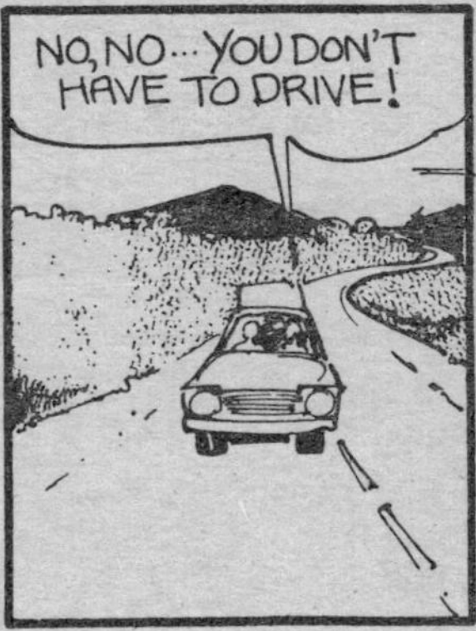
NO, NO... YOU DON'T HAVE TO DRIVE!

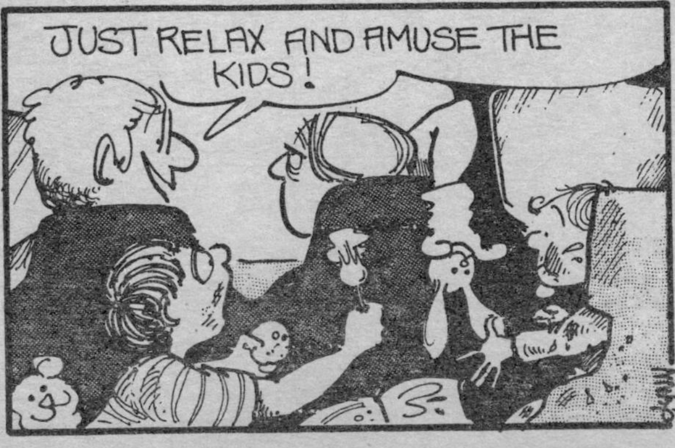
JUST RELAX AND AMUSE THE KIDS!

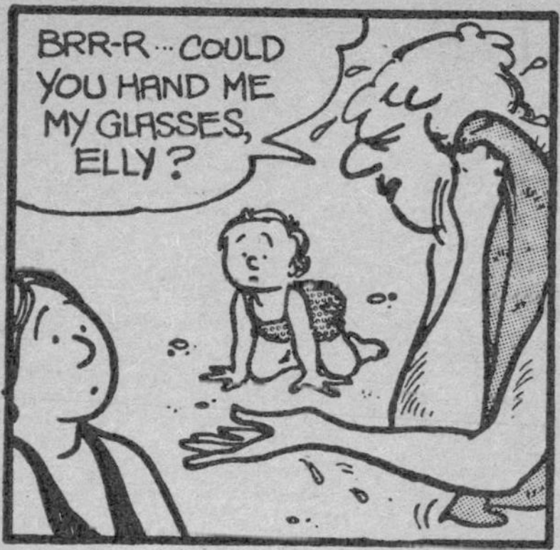
BRR-R... COULD YOU HAND ME MY GLASSES, ELLY?

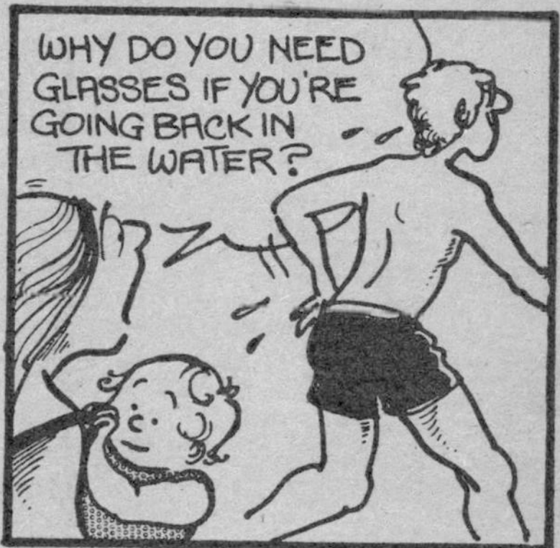
WHY DO YOU NEED GLASSES IF YOU'RE GOING BACK IN THE WATER?

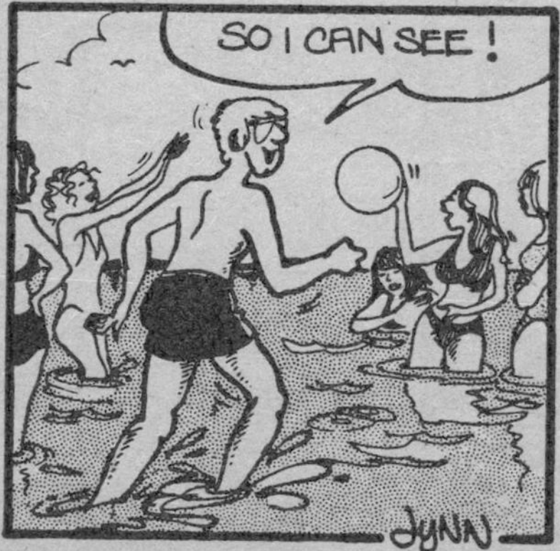
SO I CAN SEE!
LYNN

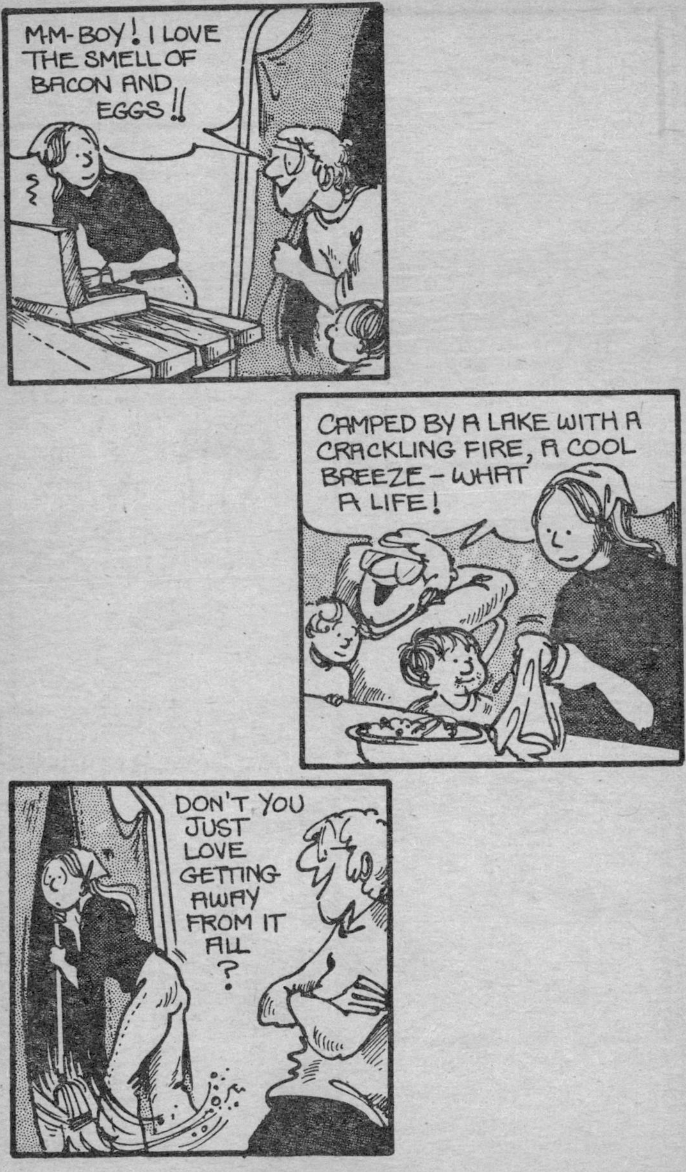
M-M-BOY! I LOVE THE SMELL OF BACON AND EGGS!!
CAMPED BY A LAKE WITH A CRACKLING FIRE, A COOL BREEZE - WHAT A LIFE!
DON'T YOU JUST LOVE GETTING AWAY FROM IT ALL?

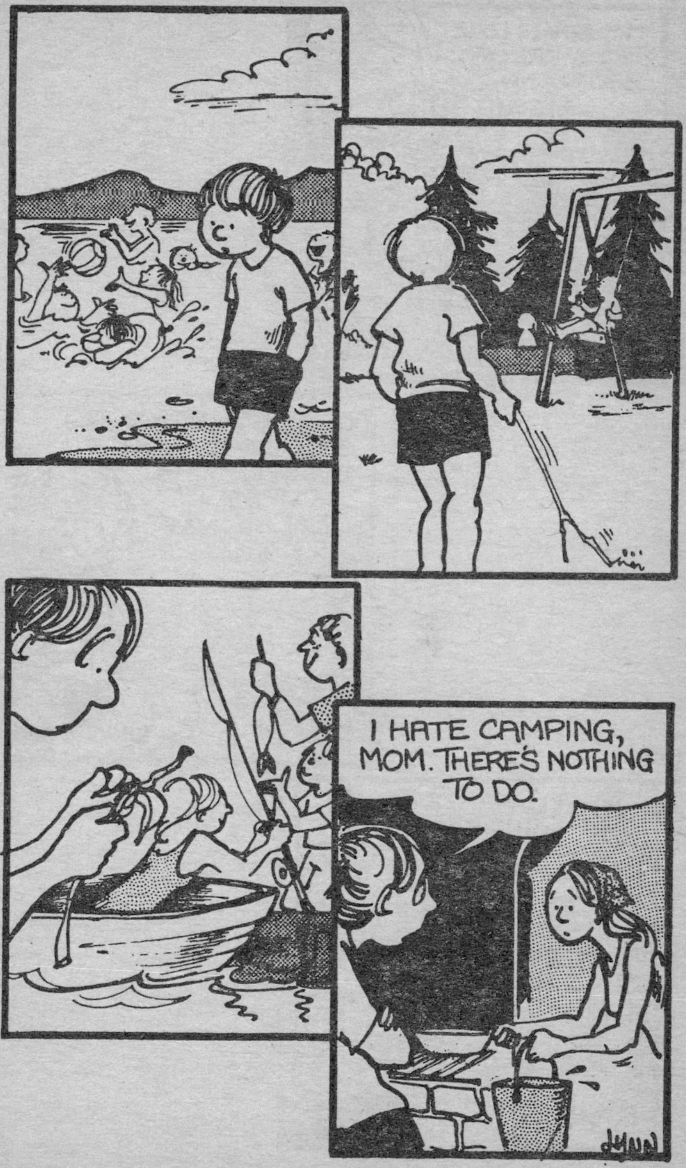
I HATE CAMPING, MOM. THERE'S NOTHING TO DO.
LYNN

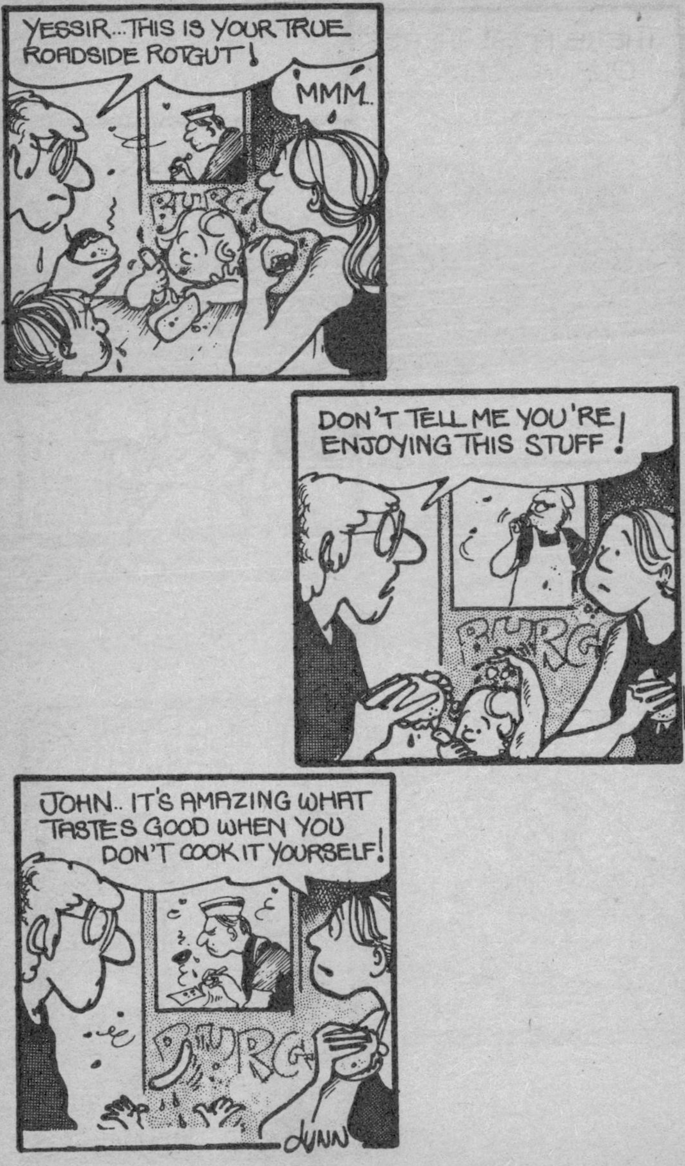
YESSIR... THIS IS YOUR TRUE ROADSIDE ROTGUT!
MMM..
DON'T TELL ME YOU'RE ENJOYING THIS STUFF!
JOHN.. IT'S AMAZING WHAT TASTES GOOD WHEN YOU DON'T COOK IT YOURSELF!
DUNN

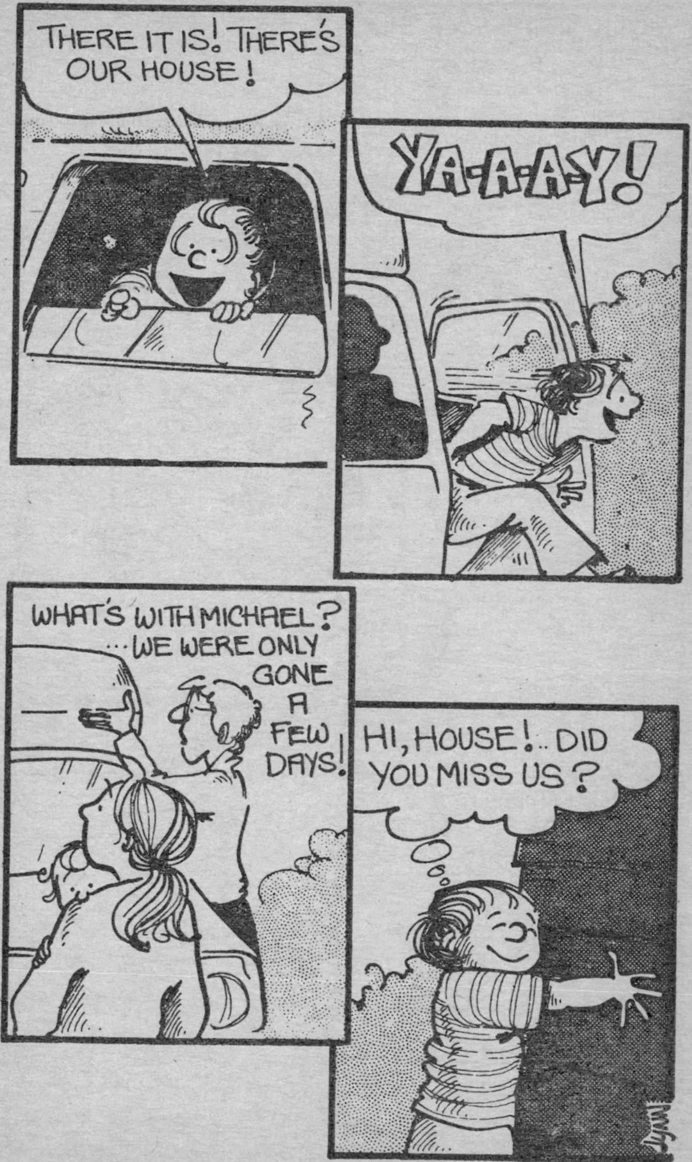
THERE IT IS! THERE'S OUR HOUSE!
YA-A-A-Y!
WHAT'S WITH MICHAEL? ...WE WERE ONLY GONE A FEW DAYS!
HI, HOUSE!.. DID YOU MISS US?

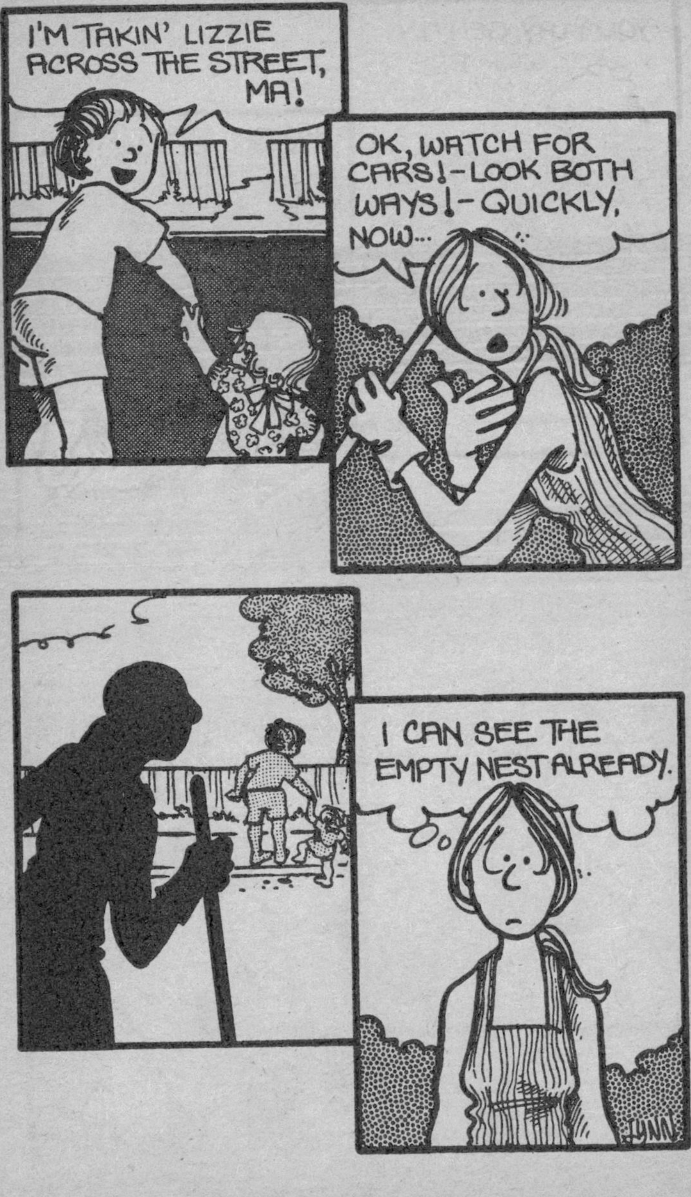
I'M TAKIN' LIZZIE ACROSS THE STREET, MA!
OK, WATCH FOR CARS!-LOOK BOTH WAYS!-QUICKLY, NOW...
I CAN SEE THE EMPTY NEST ALREADY.
LYNN

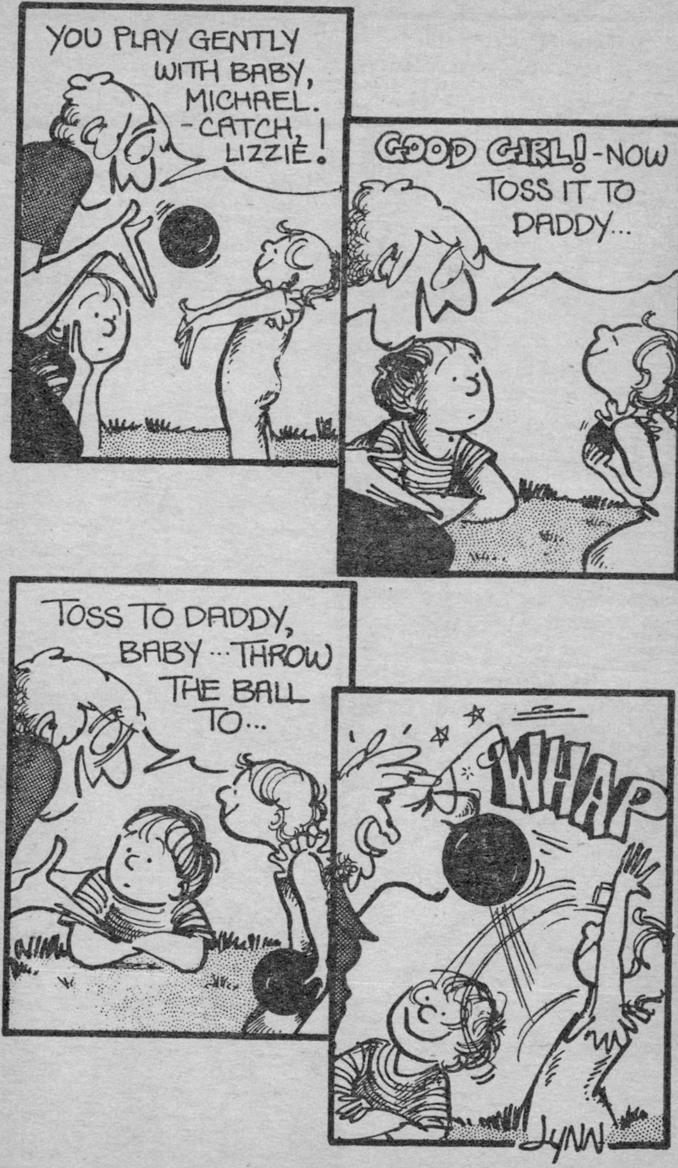
YOU PLAY GENTLY WITH BABY, MICHAEL. -CATCH, LIZZIE!
GOOD GIRL! -NOW TOSS IT TO DADDY...
TOSS TO DADDY, BABY ... THROW THE BALL TO...
WHAP
LYNN

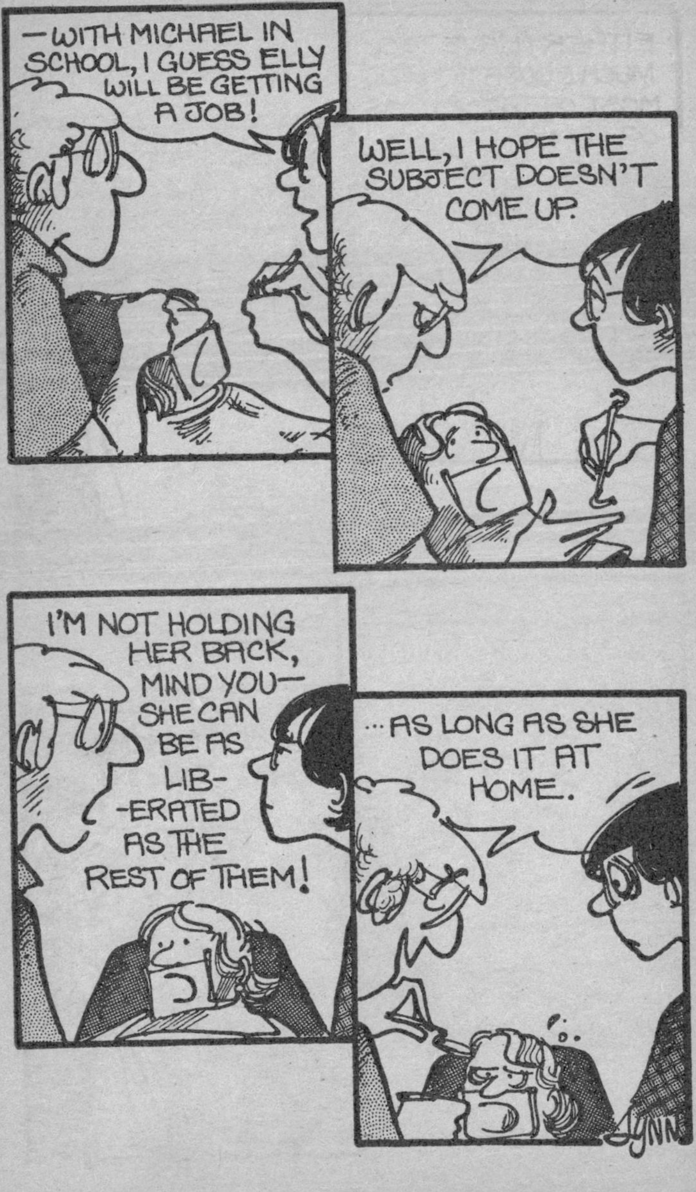
—WITH MICHAEL IN SCHOOL, I GUESS ELLY WILL BE GETTING A JOB!
WELL, I HOPE THE SUBJECT DOESN'T COME UP.
I'M NOT HOLDING HER BACK, MIND YOU— SHE CAN BE AS LIB- -ERATED AS THE REST OF THEM!
...AS LONG AS SHE DOES IT AT HOME.
LYNN

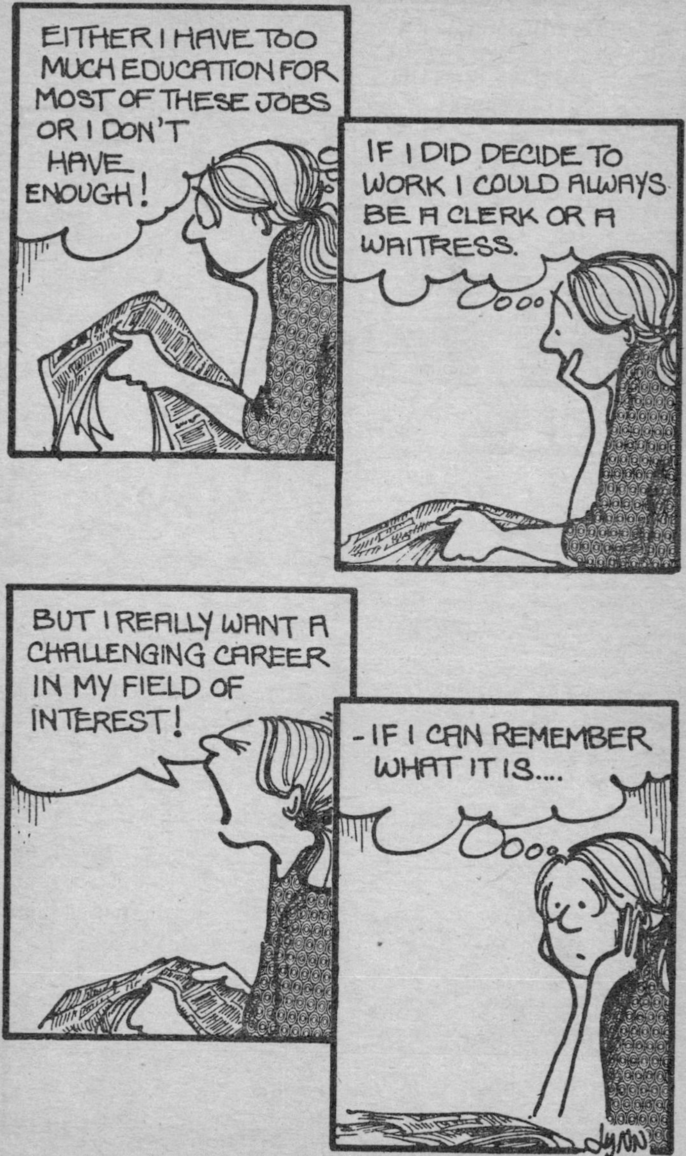
EITHER I HAVE TOO MUCH EDUCATION FOR MOST OF THESE JOBS OR I DON'T HAVE ENOUGH!
IF I DID DECIDE TO WORK I COULD ALWAYS BE A CLERK OR A WAITRESS.
BUT I REALLY WANT A CHALLENGING CAREER IN MY FIELD OF INTEREST!
-IF I CAN REMEMBER WHAT IT IS....
Lynn

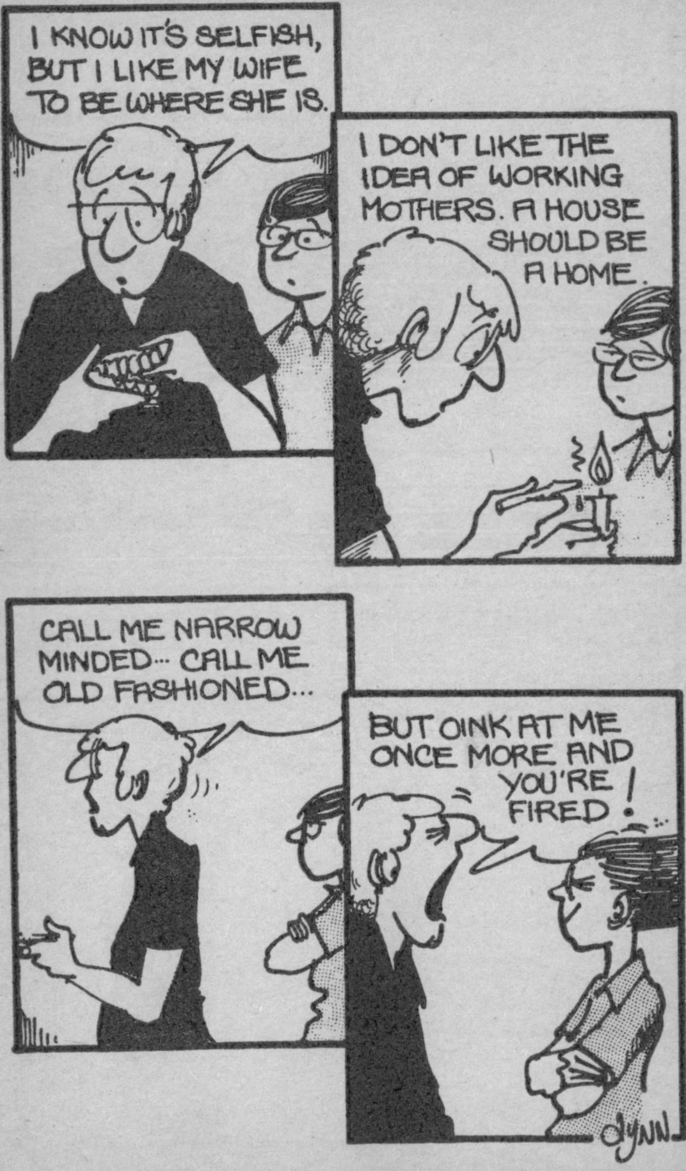
I KNOW IT'S SELFISH, BUT I LIKE MY WIFE TO BE WHERE SHE IS.
I DON'T LIKE THE IDEA OF WORKING MOTHERS. A HOUSE SHOULD BE A HOME.
CALL ME NARROW MINDED... CALL ME OLD FASHIONED...
BUT OINK AT ME ONCE MORE AND YOU'RE FIRED!
LYNN